Innovation, Social Networks, and Service Ecosystems

Jennifer D. Chandler

Innovation, Social Networks, and Service Ecosystems

Managing Value in the Digital Economy

palgrave
macmillan

Jennifer D. Chandler
California State University
Fullerton, CA, USA

ISBN 978-3-030-47796-7 ISBN 978-3-030-47797-4 (eBook)
https://doi.org/10.1007/978-3-030-47797-4

This Palgrave Macmillan imprint is published by the registered company Springer Nature Switzerland AG.
The registered company address is: Gewerbestrasse 11, 6330 Cham, Switzerland

This book is dedicated to Daniel, Jacob, and Michael. Thank you for your love and support.

Contents

Introduction

This book examines the ways in which value is created in the digital economy from a social network and service ecosystem perspective. Focusing on innovation, this project explores analytics, big data, and privacy with respect to service management and value creation. It debunks these technology-centric buzzwords by relating cross-disciplinary research topics from seminal sociology, business, management, marketing, information systems, organizational, and technology theory under the common theme of plasticity, which is the ability of a system to take and retain form. A keen understanding of plasticity is the route to success in the digital economy. This book, aimed at academics, graduate students, and practitioners in fields related to innovation, service research, and strategic management, offers a holistic perspective on innovation that is informed by scholarly research from multiple disciplines.

CHAPTER 1

Innovation from a Networked, Ecosystems Perspective

Innovation is the dilemma of the century. While it is complex and difficult to understand, innovation has been shown to be key for creating, harnessing, and managing value in the digital economy. This is because innovation is claimed to be the source or wellspring of unique and novel ideas. It is also supposed to be the key to fruitfully moving the world forward in ways that we can only imagine.

However, innovation has also become a sore spot for society as it has become a constant challenge that has become necessary for survival. Because technology is advancing at a very rapid speed, our world is now in a constant state of disruption. In our new digital economy, innovation often takes the form of technological superpowers that are based on artificial intelligence, machine learning, analytics, and big data. Together, these innovations have changed how we do business and how we conduct ourselves as human beings as we manage value in the digital economy.

Yet, it is still unclear how these will affect our society in the long term, including positive and negative effects on organizations, consumers, and government. Much of twenty-first-century technological innovations have afforded us value that we could not imagine before. We simply did not have the technology that would allow recent life-changing innovations, including, but not limited to, better treatments for illnesses, nanotechnology, energy-efficient transportation, more transparency in our governments, to name a few. Specifically, though, when it comes to organizations and the general realm of administration and business, much of the

J. D. Chandler, *Innovation, Social Networks, and Service Ecosystems*,
https://doi.org/10.1007/978-3-030-47797-4_1

innovations afforded by these new technological superpowers stem from data and data-driven devices. These data are often the basis for value in the digital economy. The data often originate from interactions on the Internet, sensors from mobile devices, cameras in public spaces, and emails in private conversations, to name a few. The data capture what human beings do on an everyday basis, including mundane transactions at the grocery store, checking out library books, paying bills, and interacting with friends and family on social media. These data are captured by organizations since they often facilitate these interactions. Within organizations, data also capture the functions that organizations execute on an everyday basis, including sales, marketing, logistics, emails, and communications via corporate websites. Data are everywhere and are being used to create value by humans, organizations, governments, and institutions. It is no wonder that these data have given rise to unprecedented innovations such as machine learning and artificial intelligence.

Despite these, as the world has become more connected than ever, we find ourselves troubled with incessant and constant connection. We are cautious at the very least about the data that we see about ourselves. When we receive an advertisement based on an email conversation that we just had ten minutes ago, we become suspicious of the organizations that surround us. In these ways, our trust is being tested. Thus, we still face the same old problem that we did in yesteryear which is about the pursuit of meaning and happiness in our everyday lives, no matter what that means for each of us. However, now we have the additional worry and opportunity of thinking about being surrounding by big data, machine learning, and artificial intelligence. This is both exciting and also somewhat scary to us human beings.

Data are scary because they share our behaviors, values, and norms with others. We ourselves may not be aware of our own behaviors, values, or norms. When data make these salient and visible, it is scary to human beings. This is because humans are innately creatures of routine, repetition, and habit. Although we value the benefits that can come from allowing our data to be available to and used by organizations, we fear the consequences of organizations owning or gaining access to this data. Sometimes, organizations and individuals may not use this data to create value for those whose behaviors and values are reflected in the data. The inherent assumption is that the data can predict future behaviors and values, since humans are creatures of habit. Although it is difficult to escape our nature of finding comfort in repetitive behaviors or habit, we do not like that our behaviors are, for the most part, predictable.

Since human beings are creatures of habit, our preferences for routine and repetition establish habits in our daily lives that are difficult to alter. They are hallmarks of our own personal comforts. Simply put, the routine behaviors give us comfort and help us to find value and meaning in our everyday lives. In the United States and other Westernized countries, people relish the certainty embedded in these routines and habits. For many human beings, their physical and mental well-being depends on the existence of routine. Because of this, it is certainly possible that the organizations that we support are collecting, housing, and harnessing data about us and our most personal daily behaviors. To a large extent, many of us enjoy how these data help our favorite organizations like Google or Apple make our lives easier; this occurs when smart devices automatically turn on lights in our houses or when our smart phones give us turn-by-turn directions as we drive to work. All the while, organizations are collecting data about our everyday lives. Many Americans and citizens of other countries are happy to share their data with companies in order to reap the value of autonomous integrations that help us to lead harmonized, simpler lives. The value, again, stems from the predictability of our behaviors, routines, and processes. Unless we can become more spontaneous and random, organizations and government can use the data to predict, inform, or even control our future behaviors.

However, the price of data and automation based on this data are not without costs. Generally speaking, we think of these technological superpowers as afforded to organizations; however, it is equally important for consumers and governments to understand these superpowers as well. The value of technology is in the data that can be easily collected and eventually harnessed via integrated devices and information systems. However, the irony is that many equate the value of digital innovation with these superpowers and the organizations associated with them. However, innovation and value do not have much to do with digital as much they have to do with problem-solving (Satell 2018). We find value when we solve problems; analogously, we innovate when we solve problems. But, because the “digital economy” is somewhat new at the time of this writing (it is the year 2020 and the Internet came into existence only 30 years ago), innovation has become the buzzword that is now interchangeable with our understanding of the digital economy. Oftentimes, innovation has become synonymous with digital economy, and vice versa.

However, as a human society, we still face the same challenges that we have always encountered since the very beginning of time. These are not necessarily digital challenges. The challenges, sadly yet somewhat gratefully, remain as simple, mundane, and analog in nature as they always have been. That is, the challenges that we face as humans are the same as they always have been: the challenges center on creating meaning in our lives. We, as human beings, are driven to innately and continuously survive; once we prove to ourselves that we can survive, we pursue meaning and happiness. These motivations have simply taken different forms over the years. For example, in the year 750, humans in China sought meaning by learning about tea-drinking, while in 1789 humans in France sought meaning by inciting political instability and uprising against their government. At the time of writing, in 2020, the humans in our world still seek meaning, but face challenges of continuing to find meaning in, or in spite of, newly introduced digital modes and formats.

This being said, the somewhat abrupt introduction of the digital economy is not going away anytime soon. As a result, it is important to understand what innovation and value entail. If we are conscious about the analysis and collection of this data, we as human beings can also use this data to improve ourselves and our worlds. If we can find the patterns that are most fundamental to finding meaning and happiness in our personal lives, the data can be harnessed for powerful value creation. Furthermore, other parts and dimensions of society that are also based in routine can benefit from the use of technology to positively influence process-oriented efforts. For example, diseases, energy use, wildlife ecology, and transportation patterns are typically also routine and process oriented. The data generated in these spaces are also reflective of patterns as well. By finding ways to harness data, it is more likely that machine learning and artificial intelligence can take a bigger role in our society, whether that role is good or bad. For all these reasons, it is important to understand innovation and value creation so we can understand how these new technological superpowers can be harnessed to benefit society.

In the big scheme of things, we are just beginning to be transformed by the digital economy. To manage this well, we need to understand how innovation and managing value in the digital economy can allow us to devise and execute new solutions to the same old problems. As stated earlier, the "same old problem" is finding meaning and happiness in our lives. From an organizational perspective, the "same old problem" would be helping our customers to find meaning in happiness in their own lives.

How do we find meaning in a world that is moving too fast? How do we find happiness when we are constantly being surveilled? How do we find solace when we are constantly inundated with new stimulus, data, and attempts to build relationships? The constraint in our powerful digital economy is the digital economy itself. As humans, we are being forced to adapt to this digital economy at an alarmingly fast rate, while we deal simultaneously with the high levels of uncertainty brought about by smartphones, social media, privacy, and endless surveillance and monitoring. Unwittingly, no one entity is forcing us as a society to move at this unparalleled speed. Rather the system itself is propagating and barreling quite quickly into the future; we are enslaved to the system while we simultaneously transform it in order to create the future that we want to see.

To move forward, we must acknowledge that we are all innovators. Companies and organizations are not the only innovators. Consumers are innovators too, as are nonprofits, governments and policy-makers. Thus, as innovators, we need time and space to uncover, unravel, and look deeper at the opportunities, challenges, and issues that come to light in the digital economy. We cannot move forward doing the same things we did in yesteryear. If we do, then we perpetuate the system as it is. We need to acknowledge that each of us is an innovator that can influence the trajectory of the system. To do this more fruitfully, we need a different lens that gives us a new way of thinking about our same old challenges with respect to the strikingly new digital opportunities facing our world. Thus, the purpose of this book is to explain innovation from a networked, ecosystems perspective so that graduate students, scholars, executives, policymakers, and managers can better understand the digital economy and how to manage value in our complex, continuously evolving environment.

What Is Innovation?

Innovation has generally been studied across disciplines as "the generation, acceptance and implementation of new ideas, processes, products, or services" (Van de Ven and Angle 1989, p. 20). Innovation is thought of as an outcome of creativity. Traditionally, innovation has been studied as a linear progression of information and knowledge. It has been known to occur as a progression through five stages: knowledge, persuasion, decision, implementation, and confirmation (Van de Ven and Angle 1989). In the knowledge phase, information is gathered and new knowledge may be generated. In the persuasion stage, others are being convinced to accept this new information or knowledge. When the new information or knowledge is accepted, the decision stage is reached. Then, the new information or knowledge is acted upon, which occurs during the implementation stage. Finally, in the confirmation stage, there is widespread acceptance of the new information and knowledge, as well as acceptance of the implementation.

Viewing innovation in this way suggests that innovation is a deliberate process that has a definitive beginning and ending. According to this viewpoint, when one stage ends, the next stage begins. Moreover, these studies suggest that innovation is about creating new knowledge, as well as garnering acceptance of that new knowledge and creating unique ideas, processes, or products based on the new knowledge (Garcia and Calantone 2003; Ordanini et al. 2013; Adner and Kapoor 2010; Clarysse et al. 2014; Dhanaraj and Parkhe 2006; Gawer and Cusumano 2013; Zahra and Nambisan 2012). Because of this, some confuse “creativity” with “innovation,” and ultimately use the two terms interchangeably. Yet, these are two terms are fundamentally different. Creativity refers to the trait of an individual; it is “an outcome (a work, a product, an idea) that is both novel and appropriate to the context or circumstance from which it arises” (Burroughs et al. 2008, p. 1011). Creativity can also refer to behaviors, thoughts, or outcomes that are *both* original and useful (Amabile 1988, 1996; Feist 1998; Guilford 1950; Runco 2004; Runco and Jaeger 2012; Simonton 2008). On the other hand, innovation relates to any and all efforts related to the generation, introduction, implementation, and acceptance of new knowledge (Shalley et al. 2004). To this end, Paruchuri (2010) thinks about innovation as “recombining and/or reconfiguring existing pieces of knowledge in some novel way” (p. 64). Many—but not all—,innovations are indeed creative, and some have become possible because of creativity; however, creativity is not necessarily an innovation and creativity does not always result from innovation.

A narrow area of innovation that relates to the digital economy focuses on innovation in service organizations. This perspective is important because it views innovation from a systems perspective that delineates all actors including organizations, consumers, and governments across society as involved in value creation. Researchers in this area refer to this as “service innovation,” a special type of innovation that requires purposive and deliberate design that can optimize the engagement of multiple types of stakeholders (e.g., employees, customers, families, and government).

Importantly, this area of research also emphasizes innovation as a continuous process that transpires across different types of landscapes and environments, including mobile user interfaces, stores, websites, restaurants and so on. A successful service innovation, for example, would encompass and facilitate successful service operations (back of the house) and delivery (front of the house) over the lifetime of the entire service experience (Bitner et al. 2015; Patrício et al. 2017; Ostrom et al. 2010, 2013; Wilden et al. 2017).

Another curious aspect of this perspective is the many-to-many involvement emphasis. Typically, service delivery is thought of as a finite occurrence at a particular moment in time. During this moment, the service encounter appears to occur between two different actors, namely a service provider and a service beneficiary. However, with the many-to-many-involvement emphasis, a service encounter can be viewed as the manifestation of many different actors' efforts that contributed to providing that exact service encounter at that particular moment in time. A many-to-many lens highlights the actions and behaviors taken by others prior to the service encounter, as well as the actions and behaviors of others after the service encounter. This all-encompassing perspective moves from emphasis on the sole service encounter as an isolated incident, to emphasizing the holistic and comprehensive service experience. By viewing service in this way, these perspectives illustrate how many different actors are actually simultaneously involved in a service encounter. Although the service encounter may occur at a moment in time, it is a smaller slice of the service experience which transcends that moment and encompasses the pre-encounter efforts and influences, as well as post-encounter efforts and influences. For the purposes of service innovation, this means thinking critically about involving the right actors in the service that would bring about the highest value for all those involved. For example, a customer might order food at a restaurant. The service encounter may include the cashier and the customer; however, the service experience would include the farmer, wholesaler, restaurant manager, chef, as well as others who are currently at the restaurant. Each of these different actors contribute to the quality and nature of the service encounter at the restaurant. Additionally, macro forces such as culture, nutrition, and lifestyle also affect the service encounter and thus can be counted as components in the service experience. Moreover, because the service experience continues after the service encounter has ended, it is necessary to consider other actors that also affect the service experience after the customer leaves the restaurant.

This might include, for example, the environment of the parking lot, the customer's car, the customer's companions to the restaurant, or even the customer's doctor if the meal was unhealthy. As can be seen, there are many different actors involved in the service encounter when viewed in this way. Any changes in the nature, number, or characteristics of these actors could change the service experience or the service encounter. Service innovation would entail thinking about how these changes might be implemented, how there is effect on the overall service experience, and ways that value can be created in a more fruitful manner.

When viewed in high-technology contexts, the same could be said for a technology-based service encounter. Take for example the service encounter of watching a video on YouTube. A service encounter would take place between a user and the YouTube website or the YouTube mobile application. However, in order for that service encounter to take place, a number of actions or behaviors would have needed to happen before the service encounter occurred. For example, the user would have had to have either an Internet connection or a mobile device that is activated on the cellular network. Also the user would need to be familiar with the YouTube website and somehow become aware of the videos existence. Among other things, an actor or actors would have had to create the video that is being watched on YouTube. They also would have needed to know how to upload the video to YouTube and have a working Internet connection. All of these together comprise the service experience. Although these are just a few examples of various segments of the service experience, it is important to note the influence of the service encounter. The service experience continues beyond the service encounter and includes other elements as well. For example, once the video has been viewed, YouTube collects data about the user and other viewers of the YouTube video. The data then becomes available for analysis and could be used for other purposes by the company. This, although unknown perhaps to the user, would be part of the service experience. Again, the data ultimately plays a fundamental role in influencing future service experiences and service encounters.

In order to innovate upon this service in particular, one might think about how the data could be collected, used, and analyzed for the user as well as the organization. Organizations may want to consider privacy and ownership issues related to the video itself or the data that is collected about the viewership. For example, deciding as to when it's appropriate to discuss privacy with the viewer would be part of the service innovation. It might also be important to consider the different types of data collection, and when it would be best to collect this data from the user. These are all aspects of the service experience to be considered during service innovation.

What Are Value Propositions and Why Are They Important?

Because the service experience is complex and multifaceted, service innovation has been identified as a difficult undertaking because successful service innovation requires the engagement of multiple actors across many smaller social systems. In order to manifest the most optimal service innovation possible, many practitioners and scholars have begun to study service innovation as a systemic process that influences, and is influenced by, the social norms, rules, and beliefs surrounding new ideas (Helkkula et al. 2018; Kurtmollaiev et al. 2017; De Benedittis 2019). This means paying close attention to the actors involved in the service encounter and service experience, along with paying close attention to the norms rules and beliefs that are associated with those actors or groups.

Because service innovation in the digital economy requires different modes of participation and the engagement of many different actors, it is fundamentally important to consider the actors and activities that are involved in or associated with service including both human and nonhuman actors. For example, when it comes to a product recommendation system, this means thinking critically about how data from past behaviors can be used to integrate new objects or recommendations into the service experience. Although this could be seen as a violation of privacy, many customers may feel that such a recommendation system could generate the highest value for all those involved. For example, a customer might stream a particular song on an online music platform. The service encounter may include the customer and the user interface; however, the service experience would include the songwriter, artist, publishing company, musicians, as well as others who were involved in the creation and distribution of the song. Each of these different actors contributes to the quality and nature of the service encounter via the music platform. Additionally, macro forces such as culture and lifestyle can influence the service encounter and should be considered in the service experience. Moreover, because the service experience continues after the service encounter has ended, it is necessary to consider other actors that may influence the service experience after the song has finished streaming. This might include, for example, an online interview with the artist, mentions of the songwriter on social media, the customer's musical tastes, or even the customer's other playlists. As can be seen, there are many different actors involved in the service experience when viewed in this way. Any changes in the nature, number, or characteristics of these actors could change the service experience or the service encounter.

Because we are all innovators and we all pursue value creation, or the generation of beneficial outcomes, we all have the choice to become involved in many different service experiences. Thus, it is important to involve the appropriate actors in a service experience in order for it to be successful. There has always been significant emphasis on organizational efforts and outcomes related to value creation. However, humans are the ones creating the value, and they do this together in groups often within organizations. Humans are always involved in value creation, and oftentimes consumers are involved in value creation in ways that are not always known to the organization that originates the item in the first place. Humans work toward creating value, for example when they organize a shipment of lumber in the stockroom of a home repair shop and then place these pieces of lumber on a store shelf for display. Then, for example, another human (i.e., a consumer) works toward creating value when she examines and subsequently purchases a piece of lumber at the home repair shop. In theory, value is supposed to have been created at that point of transaction. Yet, that piece of lumber only has value to the consumer when the lumber is used for home repairs or to assemble a table at home. The item is not valuable without the consumer.

Thinking about value creation in this way essentially entails service innovation—thinking about how all these human processes can be brought together within the service experience (Chase and Apte 2006). For example, it is often thought that organizations are the originators of items that are created and sold. Although many different types of organizations play varying roles in creating and selling these items, the items are thought of as "valuable" because it was thought that the items themselves innately have "value." But, value is not something embedded in things (Holbrook 1994). Rather, value is created when these things become engaged in different processes, routines, or activities that generate beneficial outcomes for humans (Vargo and Lusch 2004, 2007; Normann and Ramirez 1998).

Thinking about service innovation requires viewing these as an amalgamation of these processes that together can bring humans together jointly over time.

To involve varying types of actors in service, value propositions are offered from one actor to one another. Stated differently, value propositions are invitations from actors to one another to engage in a service experience. Because of this, value propositions have been studied as proposed solutions (Teece 2010; Zott et al. 2011; Fleury and Fleury 2014). They help actors to either explain or understand how a service experience can solve a problem or address a particular challenge (Bolton et al. 2004). With respect to service innovation, a value proposition can "become a starting point for negotiation, or an agenda for working together with participating stakeholders to create mutual benefits" (Ballantyne et al. 2011, p. 205). The value proposition begins the conversation for negotiating innovation. In other words, value propositions act as starting points for value creation since they can bring actors together for service innovation. Because actors are continually offering, evaluating, and accepting value propositions, all actors are always simultaneously joining, rejecting, and starting service experiences. We are together in a continuous dialogue about to best create value for ourselves and others. A compelling value proposition invites the appropriate actors to participate in service experience in such a way that value can be created.

In the digital economy, it has become challenging to offer, evaluate, and accept value propositions because there are many varying, sometimes conflicting, views on beneficial outcomes (Sewell 1992). This is especially true for Internet-of-Things (IoT) settings where "the interconnection of uniquely identifiable embedded computing devices" is transforming services processes among machines, objects, and humans (Scoble et al. 2014). Likewise, artificial intelligence and big data are also changing service processes and raising challenges related to online spaces, privacy, and data ownership. It is difficult to advance compelling value propositions in this space because the needs and wants of customers differ greatly. For many, their preferences, needs and wants are largely unknown because it has not been previously necessary to be fully aware of these (Anderson et al. 2006). Many customers are not aware of their needs and wants. Others are not aware of the implications or consequences of their needs and wants. For example, while some actors do not hesitate to share their emotions and sentiments on social media, other actors rarely investigate other news sources beyond their routine social media pages to validate reports of current events. Likewise, some actors are happy to share their information in online spaces and will willingly give an organization their credit card numbers. Meanwhile, other actors refuse to use online banking and other online financial services because of their suspicion of online privacy and theft. Based on these varying preferences, value propositions are offered in these spaces from many different actors. In response, the invited actors have the unique power to evaluate, reject, or accept these value propositions. Because of the sheer volume of value propositions being proposed all the time, it is not necessary or even encouraged to evaluate or let alone accept all value propositions. This is especially true since many actors play many roles that can be influenced by a single value proposition. For these reasons, it is important to be mindful and discerning about the evaluation, rejection, and/or acceptance of value propositions since this largely determines with which service processes they will ultimately be engaged. Many actors can do this better when they are mindful and aware of their embeddedness in social networks.

Since innovation and value creation are thus largely collaborative efforts as described above, it can be helpful to think about them as taking place within social groups, or social networks. To explore this, I invoke social theory and, specifically, social networks analysis (SNA) (Wasserman and Faust 1994). SNA is the study of social structure and involves the quantitative analysis of relational datasets (Borgatti et al. 2018; Wellman and Berkowitz 1996). SNA is built on "snapshots" of social structures at a moment in time; because of this, many sociometric measures represent particular moments from the past. Chandler and Vargo (2011) began to use SNA to propose a framework for exploring value creation from a social networks analysis perspective by identifying context as a "set of unique actors with unique reciprocal links among them" (p. 40). That set of actors and the links among them exist at that particular moment in time. The authors further assert that these moments of time can be better understood by zooming in and zooming out on specific processes. They assert that it is necessary to oscillate foci from a one-on-one level (i.e., micro-level) to an organizational level (i.e., meso level) and societal level (i.e., macro level), and then back again. Such an approach helps to make salient the simultaneous influences of micro, meso, and macro factors in the service experience, and their influences on value creation and innovation on a service encounter at a particular moment in time. Accordingly, each level is described below.

A micro-level perspective focuses on individuals and their relationships with one another at a particular moment in time. This means that a micro-level perspective also emphasizes dyads, or each set of individuals that are connected by a relationship between them (Wasserman and Faust 1994). Accordingly, one specific individual can be a member of many dyads since that individual may have multiple relationships with many individuals at a particular moment in time. The relationships may neither be necessarily reciprocal nor mutual. For example, the relationship can consist of advice-seeking or advice-giving between two people. In a high-technology environment, however, the relationship may exist between a periphery device and an operating system; in other words, one may be receiving directions while the other may be giving directions. It is important that each type of behavior may occur in one direction or the other, and the relationship is not always reciprocal at a particular moment in time. However, other relationships such as friendship, can be mutual, with the relationship extending in both directions from one individual to the other. Reciprocal relationships are especially important for value creation because the symmetry of these relationships often entails that both individuals are providing value for the other, at a particular moment in time. This is especially important in a high-technology environment where systems must be resilient and be able to respond to change from either individuals and their relationships. The strength of these relationships are important for innovation and value creation because these close, tight bonds are likely to aid the persistence of the beneficial outcomes that are associated with innovation.

A meso-level perspective focuses on groups, teams, and organizations. In a high-technology environment, the meso-level perspective can focus on or a subgroup of process-based operations. This means that a meso-level perspective also emphasizes online communities and other groups of actors that tend to interact regularly at a particular moment in time. Individuals in these groupings are often connected to one another and, as such, influence one another at a particular moment in time. In this way, these groups enhance stability and provide mechanisms that efficiently allow for the diffusion of new information or novel, unique ideas, and behaviors. Some of these groups consist of individuals who are similar to one another in that they share similar characteristics such as backgrounds, interests, experiences, and traits. Because of this, groups may share social norms and thus reinforce values or beliefs that tend to shape and influence individual opinions, preferences, and behaviors to coincide with those of the others in the group. In high-technology environments, such groups can form around accepted protocols that are industrywide or generation specific. An example of this would be a lightning cable or an analog sound cable. When such subgroups are fundamental to keeping an ecosystem intact, they provide more cohesion but cannot also limit the resilience of the ecosystem as industry protocols change or as next-generation technology advances. Despite this, other groups can be relatively heterogeneous and thus exert less influence on their members. In high-technology environment, this can be seen in open-source software systems or in open-source application development platforms. It is been argued that such heterogeneous subgrouping can make the overall ecosystem more resilient; however, it has also been argued that such heterogeneity can also at the same time render the overall ecosystem more vulnerable to outside influence. Nonetheless, the relationships in these groups act as conduits for the diffusion of new technologies, ideas, or behaviors to others in the wider ecosystem. This perspective is important for innovation and value creation because these groups aid in the acceptance and/or rejection of new ideas and technologies, as well as implementations thereof.

A macro-level perspective focuses on large masses of individuals such as in societies, industries, and populations. This means that a macro-level perspective also emphasizes institutions, density, and overall structures at a particular moment in time (Wasserman and Faust 1994). A common feature of large groups is a "core" of highly active individuals surrounded by more peripheral, less active members. This is called a core–periphery structure in which the center of a large group is a tightly connected, cohesive set of individuals who have deep connections with one another. Meanwhile, this core is surrounded by other individuals who are loosely connected to one another and the core. This is the periphery. The institutional logics literature focuses on how these large groups influence, and are influenced by, other large groups at a particular moment in time. A macro-level perspective might emphasize the commonalities that are designed into products by their manufacturers. Such commonalities can make consumer products more compatible with one another, which lays the ground for entire ecosystems of products to coalesce in the market. A nether macro-level perspective includes that of consumer sentiment around online privacy. In some places, online privacy is more important, while in other places the sharing of information is more important. This is the influence of culture on technology, and this perspective is important for innovation and value creation because these large groups confirm the acceptance of new ideas and implementations.

To clarify how these perspectives can help to better understand innovation and value creation, it is helpful to draw a metaphorical comparison between innovation and water. Imagine that innovation is water. Each of these perspectives focuses on water with a different amplitude of magnification. The magnification level can be either at the teaspoon level, where water is viewed as droplets (i.e., micro level), at the glass level, where water is viewed as glass of water droplets (i.e., meso level), or at the atmosphere level, where water is viewed as humidity, rain, or snow consisting of water droplets (macro level). All the droplets are water, but there is simply a different number of droplets at each perspective or magnification level. Nonetheless, each is a unique perspective on the same water and each perspective hones in on different properties, traits, or dynamics of the water. This is similar to what we can see when we use a telescope versus the naked eye to look at the night sky, or when we use a microscope versus the naked eye to look at plant cells in a petri dish.

Understanding these varying levels of magnification is important for understanding innovation and value creation because innovation and value creation occur simultaneously at the micro, meso, and macro levels among, respectively, individuals and dyads, groups and organizations, as well institutions and societies. The micro "individual level of value" is not isolated from a macro "collective level of value." The micro level is embedded within a meso level, which is itself embedded simultaneously in a macro level; each level is a different magnification of the same phenomenon (Chandler and Vargo 2011). The meso level focuses on a collective, intersection, or relation of an individual, while the micro level focuses on the individual itself and the macro level focuses on the environment in which the meso and micro levels exist. Thus, the meso level points attention to ecosystem "subsystems" that interconnect micro and meso levels of value.

Time and Innovation

These perspectives help us to move from the traditional view of innovation that emphasizes only the service encounter, or the micro-level one-to-one interaction. Because we are all connected, it is important to a move toward a more comprehensive view that also incorporates the larger systems behind and beyond micro-level interactions at a particular moment in time so that we can better understand the service experience. Individual actors seldom behave in isolation from their own cultures, macro-level influences, or influences from family and friends. Moreover, it is often proposed that past behaviors are the best predictors of future behaviors. Relatedly, past interactions can generate an accumulated effect on present moments. Together, they often contribute and give rise to innovation. Based on this, it is clear that innovation does not come into existence in one instance; innovation is an accumulation of past interactions.

To explore this further, it is necessary to discuss the roles of time and temporality. In each instance of value creation, individuals, groups, and institutions are involved at that particular moment of time in the service encounter. Analogously, in each service encounter, individuals, groups, and institutions beyond the dyad are, were, or will be involved beyond that particular moment of time. In that moment, each of these perspectives, which represent different levels of magnification on a service experience, can be obtained by zooming our focus in and out on those involved in innovation.

However, in order to better understand innovation and value creation, it is important to recognize that there are many simultaneous interactions among many different actors that give rise to a single moment. This is why it is important to differentiate the service encounter from the service experience. Simply stated, there is always a history of interactions that precedes innovation or value creation. Similarly, there are also many series of imminent interactions, or futures, that follow from each of these interactions. The entire string of past, present, and future interactions coalesces into systems that are "nonlinear and highly dynamic and involve multiple agencies, institutions, organizations, communities and individuals (Maull et al. 2012, page 72)." These systems are always fleeting and dynamically changing, and their shadows constantly evolve. The systems are important because they often precede innovation. Within each system, a meta-layer is a temporal trajectory upon which the micro, meso, and macro levels move continuously together through time. Each micro, meso, and macro system moves along the meta-layer in a jointly interlocked evolution, much like fabrics slide together along a thread. Interactions ring throughout the system, as the meta-layer twists, stretches, and contracts in response to past interactions, while simultaneously morphing future interactions. Each interaction, thus, can fundamentally change the meta-layer. When this happens, innovation occurs.

When taking this perspective on innovation, it is important to extend how we think about innovation. Innovation has traditionally been studied as a linear process that typically culminates in a successful outcome. It would be wonderful if we could all succeed at innovation on our first attempt! Innovation, though, is the rise and fall of many related processes, some of which build upon one another despite failure. Together these various processes ultimately give rise to a successful outcome at a later time. In other words, failures are not typically failed innovations; rather, failures are almost always the efforts that bring us one step closer to successful outcomes that look like innovation. All the failures should be included in the innovation yet we typically ignore the failures and highlight only the successes when we talk about innovation. Remember that innovation is about problem-solving. Failures help us to better understand the problems that we are to solve. As such, failures are early-stage successes because they help to shape the future interactions necessary for innovation to occur.

Thinking Service Ecosystems

Because of this, value propositions are extremely important, since at each particular moment of time every individual actor evaluates and then can accept or reject a value proposition. In other words, at every moment of time, an individual can join or depart from an ongoing innovation process. It is impossible to predict which of these actors can be pivotal to innovation!

When it comes to high-technology environments for example, consider a periphery device that is connected to an operating system. The periphery device offers a value proposition to the operating system in that the device can send new information (as input) to the operating system. The operating system can accept or reject the value proposition. This begins with the compatibility between the device in the operating system; that is, if the two are not compatible enough, the value proposition is rejected and any new information or interoperability offered by the device is rejected by the system. However, if the two are indeed compatible, then the value proposition is accepted by the operating system. Moreover, it is more probable that new information or interoperability offered by the device can influence the system successfully in some way.

In another example with respect to data warehouses, the designer of the database sets up the parameters for the data to be accepted in a particular format. This can be viewed as the logic of the database. When the new data enter the database, they should be formatted to meet the parameters of the database. The new data appear as a value proposition. If the data are not formatted appropriately, the database or the system rejects the data and the data cannot be accepted into the data warehouse. On the other hand, if the data are formatted appropriately, the database in the system are more willing to accept the data and the associated value proposition of the data. The data can be more readily accepted into the data warehouse and the wider ecosystem.

At every moment of time, any value propositions like these are being offered across multiple service ecosystems. As a result, in every moment of time, there is a consequence that is translated into the meta-layer as it reverberates at each of the three levels. If there are tensions or divergences, there are consequences at the micro, meso, and macro levels. Similarly, if there are beneficial outcomes, there are also consequences at the micro, meso, and macro levels. Thus, value propositions are fundamentally important to value creation because they invite different actors to participate or join an innovation process and each individual may enhance, detract from, or transform the innovation process. Consider, for example, the infection of a virus into an operating system. The virus may appear initially as new information or new interoperability that seems appealing to the system. However, once the virus has been accepted, it can substantially detract from or transform the entire system. In many cases viruses have even destroyed entire operating systems. For this reason, it is not surprising that many service ecosystems are built to be stable and closed, in order to enhance security against certain types of value propositions.

Likewise, when different individuals depart from or leave service ecosystem, their departure may enhance, detract, or transform the innovation process. In this way, innovation can be seen to occur within a service ecosystem, or a "relatively self-contained, self-adjusting system of resource-integrating actors connected by shared institutional logics and mutual value creation through service exchange". By thinking about service ecosystems, it becomes fundamental to note that value creation does not occur because of any one single actor. It occurs when many actors are joined together for some positive outcome. Sometimes the actors are aware that they're joined together, while other times they are not aware of their embeddedness in a lighter system. Furthermore, it is not always possible for all actors who are involved in an ecosystem to be aware of or conscious of the outcome, let alone whether it is positive or negative for themselves and or for others. When the pasts and futures of individuals are tied together in the meta-layer, these individuals become embedded in synchronized service ecosystems and become reliant on others in the system to survive and thrive (Vargo et al. 2008). In this way, there is implicit coordination and collaboration among these individual actors. Oftentimes, these individuals come to share the same values and beliefs. From this, it can be surmised that institutional logics, or socially constructed patterns of material practices by which actors organize themselves, influence and shape interactions in these systems (Thornton and Ocasio 1999). Institutions, or "those routinized, coordinating mechanisms of various types, and *institutional arrangements*, assemblages of interdependent institutions become essential to understanding value co-creation" (Vargo and Lusch 2015, emphasis in original). In high-technology environments, these institutions might not directly influence the technological devices, hardware, or software; rather, institutions influence the coders and designers that create these technological items. For example, when industrywide protocols such as a micro USB cord exist to improve hardware compatibility, the institutional arrangements surrounding the design, manufacturing, and distribution of such cords might determine the prevalence of this cord type across service ecosystems. It should be noted that service ecosystems can be hybrid in their makeup of both human and technological actors, for example the mix of both customer service agents and ATM machines at financial service institutions such as banks. Humans who are involved in the design and coding of the technology are influenced by the culture and institutions that surround them.

When service ecosystems are aligned, value creation is stable and consistent. This can be seen, for example, in the illustration above, where an industry standard dictates the use of a micro USB cord, and also in the US education system, which has long been established on 12 years of education and formal schooling. However, when service ecosystems are not aligned, there is less value creation in the current moment. Sometimes divergent institutional logics disrupt value creation (Thornton and Ocasio 1999). Sometimes the contrasting desires or wants of specific actors introduce competing institutional logics into a service ecosystem. Different principles for value creation might arise that begin new opportunities or make way for unique, novel ways of thinking (Christensen et al. 2020). Sometimes this leads to more value creation (Akaka et al. 2013).

Scholarly Takeaway

The scholarly takeaway from this chapter is that innovation is all about problem-solving. Moreover, in this chapter we outlined that our problems in today's digital economy are the same problems that we had in yesteryear when our problems were all still analog. Simply put, the good news is that we are still human. However, we are facing a society that is changing at an alarmingly fast rate due to constant advances in technology. Our biggest constraint in the digital economy is the digital economy itself. We have become embedded in service ecosystems that transcend space and time. It's difficult to make sense of this embeddedness, especially when we are continually faced with invitations to engage, or value proposition. It is necessary to look at ourselves as innovators and to view innovation as a networked, systemic phenomena. When we do this, our role and the role of technology can be clearer. In short, this means viewing innovation at different magnifications, as it occurs simultaneously on multiple levels. This also means viewing innovation as a nonlinear temporal phenomenon that extends beyond the moment when a dyadic service encounter occurs.

Managerial Takeaway

From a managerial perspective, the takeaway from this chapter is, again, that we are still human. This means that innovation happens for us on an everyday level, in ways that we often don't see or think about it because they involve behavioral norms, values, and beliefs. When it comes to data collection, for example, and privacy, it could be as simple is becoming a little more discerning about social media about the conversations that we have every day with our customers. As a manager working in this space, we can be a little more mindful about how we discuss data, data analytics, and artificial intelligence. After all we are indeed still humans pursuing meaning and happiness. How can technology help us to do that in a digital economy? The answer to this question will give us better clues about managing value in the digital economy.

References

Adner, Ron, and Rahul Kapoor. 2010. Value Creation in Innovation Ecosystems: How the Structure of Technological Interdependence Affects Firm Performance in New Technology Generations. *Strategic Management Journal* 31 (3): 306–333. https://doi.org/10.1002/smj.821.

Akaka, Melissa Archpru, et al. 2013. The Complexity of Context: A Service Ecosystems Approach for International Marketing. *Journal of International Marketing* 21 (4): 1–20. https://doi.org/10.1509/jim.13.0032.

Amabile, Teresa M. 1988. A Model of Creativity and Innovation in Organizations. *Research in Organizational Behavior*, 1st ed., 10, JAI Press Inc, 123–167.

———. 1996. Creativity and Innovation in Organizations. *Harvard Business School Background Note*, January: 396–239.

Anderson, James C, et al. 2006. Customer Value Propositions in Business Markets. *Harvard Business Review*, March.

Ballantyne, David, et al. 2011. Value Propositions as Communication Practice: Taking a Wider View. *Industrial Marketing Management* 40 (2): 202–210. https://doi.org/10.1016/j.indmarman.2010.06.032.

Bitner, Mary Jo, et al. 2015. Journal of Service Research Special Issue on Service Design and Innovation. *Journal of Service Research* 18 (1): 3–3. https://doi.org/10.1177/1094670514557193.

Bolton, Ruth N., et al. 2004. The Theoretical Underpinnings of Customer Asset Management: A Framework and Propositions for Future Research. *Journal of the Academy of Marketing Science* 32 (3): 271–292. https://doi.org/10.1177/0092070304263341.

Borgatti, Stephen P., et al. 2018. *Analyzing Social Networks*. London: Sage.

Burroughs, James E., et al. 2008. Toward a Psychology of Consumer Creativity. *Handbook of Consumer Psychology*: 1011–1038. https://doi.org/10.4324/9780203809570.ch40.

Chandler, Jennifer D., and Stephen L. Vargo. 2011. Contextualization and Value-in-Context: How Context Frames Exchange. *Marketing Theory* 11 (1): 35–49. https://doi.org/10.1177/1470593110393713.

Chase, Richard B., and Uday M. Apte. 2006. A History of Research in Service Operations: What's the Big Idea? *Journal of Operations Management* 25 (2): 375–386. https://doi.org/10.1016/j.jom.2006.11.002.

Christensen, Clayton M., et al. 2020. Marketing Malpractice: The Cause and the Cure. *Harvard Business Review*, March 2. hbr.org/2005/12/marketing-malpractice-the-cause-and-the-cure

Clarysse, Bart, et al. 2014. Creating Value in Ecosystems: Crossing the Chasm Between Knowledge and Business Ecosystems. *Research Policy* 43 (7): 1164–1176. https://doi.org/10.1016/j.respol.2014.04.014.

De Benedittis, Julien. 2019. Transition Between Temporary Organizations: Dimensions Enabling Economies of Recombination. *International Journal of Project Management* 37 (7): 912–929. https://doi.org/10.1016/j.ijproman.2019.07.003.

Dhanaraj, Charles, and Arvind Parkhe. 2006. Orchestrating Innovation Networks. *Academy of Management Review* 31 (3): 659–669. https://doi.org/10.5465/amr.2006.21318923.

Feist, Gregory J. 1998. A Meta-Analysis of Personality in Scientific and Artistic Creativity. *Personality and Social Psychology Review* 2 (4): 290–309. https://doi.org/10.1207/s15327957pspr0204_5.

Fleury, Afonso, and Maria Tereza Leme Fleury. 2014. Local Enablers of Business Models: The Experience of Brazilian Multinationals Acquiring in North America. *Journal of Business Research* 67 (4): 516–526. https://doi.org/10.1016/j.jbusres.2013.11.008.

Garcia, Rosanna, and Roger Calantone. 2003. A Critical Look at Technological Innovation Typology and Innovativeness Terminology: A Literature Review. *Journal of Product Innovation Management* 19 (2): 110–132. https://doi.org/10.1111/1540-5885.1920110.

Gawer, Annabelle, and Michael A. Cusumano. 2013. Industry Platforms and Ecosystem Innovation. *Journal of Product Innovation Management* 31 (3): 417–433. https://doi.org/10.1111/jpim.12105.

Guilford, J.P. 1950. Creativity. *American Psychologist* 5 (9): 444–454. https://doi.org/10.1037/h0063487.

Helkkula, Anu, et al. 2018. Archetypes of Service Innovation. *Journal of Service Research* 21 (3): 284–301. https://doi.org/10.1177/1094670517746776.

Holbrook, Morris B. 1994. The Nature of Customer Value: An Axiology of Services in the Consumption Experience. *Service Quality: New Directions in Theory and Practice* 21–71. https://doi.org/10.4135/9781452229102.n2

Kurtmollaiev, Seidali, et al. 2017. Organizational Transformation Through Service Design. *Journal of Service Research* 21 (1): 59–74. https://doi.org/10.1177/1094670517738371.

Maull, Roger, et al. 2012. Service Supply Chains: A Customer Perspective. *Journal of Supply Chain Management* 48 (4): 72–86. https://doi.org/10.1111/j.1745-493x.2012.03284.x.

Normann, Richard, and Rafael Ramirez. 1998. *Designing Interactive Strategy: From Value Chain to Value Constellation.* Chichester: John Wiley & Sons.

Ordanini, Andrea, et al. 2013. When the Recipe Is More Important Than the Ingredients. *Journal of Service Research* 17 (2): 134–149. https://doi.org/10.1177/1094670513513337.

Ostrom, Amy L., et al. 2010. Moving Forward and Making a Difference: Research Priorities for the Science of Service. *Journal of Service Research* 13 (1): 4–36. https://doi.org/10.1177/1094670509357611.

Paruchuri, Srikanth. 2010. Intraorganizational Networks, Interorganizational Networks, and the Impact of Central Inventors: A Longitudinal Study of Pharmaceutical Firms. *Organization Science* 21 (1): 63–80. https://doi.org/10.1287/orsc.1080.0414.

Patrício, Lia, et al. 2017. Upframing Service Design and Innovation for Research Impact. *Journal of Service Research* 21 (1): 3–16. https://doi.org/10.1177/1094670517746780.

Runco, Mark A. 2004. Everyone Has Creative Potential. *Creativity: From Potential to Realization* 21–30. https://doi.org/10.1037/10692-002.

Runco, Mark A., and Garrett J. Jaeger. 2012. The Standard Definition of Creativity. *Creativity Research Journal* 24 (1): 92–96. https://doi.org/10.1080/10400419.2012.650092.

Satell, Greg. 2018. 4 Ways to Build an Innovative Team. *Harvard Business Review*, Harvard Business Publishing, February 13. hbr.org/2018/02/4-ways-to-build-an-innovative-team

Scoble, Robert, et al. 2014. *Age of Context: Mobile, Sensors, Data and the Future of Privacy*. Scotts Valley, CA: Patrick Brewster Press.

Sewell, William H. 1992. A Theory of Structure: Duality, Agency and Transformation. *American Journal of Sociology* 98 (1): 1–29. https://doi.org/10.1086/229967.

Shalley, Christina E., et al. 2004. The Effects of Personal and Contextual Characteristics on Creativity: Where Should We Go from Here? *Journal of Management* 30 (6): 933–958. https://doi.org/10.1016/j.jm.2004.06.007.

Simonton, Dean Keith. 2008. Scientific Talent, Training, and Performance: Intellect, Personality, and Genetic Endowment. *Review of General Psychology* 12 (1): 28–46. https://doi.org/10.1037/1089-2680.12.1.28.

Teece, David J. 2010. Business Models, Business Strategy and Innovation. *Long Range Planning* 43 (2–3): 172–194. https://doi.org/10.1016/j.lrp.2009.07.003.

Thornton, Patricia H., and William Ocasio. 1999. Institutional Logics and the Historical Contingency of Power in Organizations: Executive Succession in the Higher Education Publishing Industry, 1958–1990. *American Journal of Sociology* 105 (3): 801–843. https://doi.org/10.1086/210361.

Van de Ven, Andrew H., and Harold L. Angle. 1989. *Suggestions for Managing the Innovation Journey*. Minneapolis: Strategic Management Research Center, University of Minnesota.

Vargo, Stephen L., and Robert F. Lusch. 2004. Evolving to a New Dominant Logic for Marketing. *Journal of Marketing* 68 (1): 1–17. https://doi.org/10.1509/jmkg.68.1.1.24036.

———. 2007. Service-Dominant Logic: Continuing the Evolution. *Journal of the Academy of Marketing Science* 36 (1): 1–10. https://doi.org/10.1007/s11747-007-0069-6.

———. 2015. Institutions and Axioms: An Extension and Update of Service-Dominant Logic. *Journal of the Academy of Marketing Science* 44 (1): 5–23. https://doi.org/10.1007/s11747-015-0456-3.

Vargo, Stephen L., et al. 2008. On Value and Value Co-creation: A Service Systems and Service Logic Perspective. *European Management Journal* 26 (3): 145–152. https://doi.org/10.1016/j.emj.2008.04.003.

Wasserman, Stanley, and Katherine Louise Milton Faust. 1994. *Social Network Analysis: Methods and Applications.* Cambridge: Cambridge University Press.

Wellman, Barry, and Stephen D. Berkowitz. 1996. *Social Structures: A Network Approach.* Norwood: Ablex Pub.

Wilden, Ralf, et al. 2017. The Evolution and Prospects of Service-Dominant Logic. *Journal of Service Research* 20 (4): 345–361. https://doi.org/10.1177/1094670517715121.

Zahra, Shaker A., and Satish Nambisan. 2012. Entrepreneurship and Strategic Thinking in Business Ecosystems. *Business Horizons* 55 (3): 219–229. https://doi.org/10.1016/j.bushor.2011.12.004.

Zott, Christoph, et al. 2011. The Business Model: Recent Developments and Future Research. *SSRN Electronic Journal*, May 2. https://doi.org/10.2139/ssrn.1674384

CHAPTER 2

Plasticity: Toward a Better Understanding of Innovation

In Chap. 1, we discussed innovation and traditional definitions of innovation. Hopefully you were convinced to view innovation as a networked, systemic process that goes beyond the single outcome that is often highlighted as innovation. I also highlighted that multiple interactions must transpire in order for innovation to take root and prosper. Sometimes these interactions might look like failures, but, in actuality, they often set the stage for a subsequent successful outcome.

Because most studies of innovation focus only on that unique outcome, idea, or solution that is publicly successful, these studies largely ignore the dynamic systems that give rise to innovation as a broad encompassing process. In order to harness value in the digital economy, we cannot afford to ignore these interactions; they are as important as the successful outcomes themselves. The seemingly failed outcomes and the seemingly failed interactions help us to frame the problem in a way that makes a plausible solution possible (Patrício et al. 2017). In the same way, we must not ignore the interactions that take place or transpire outside of the dyadic service encounters on which we often focus; these interactions that take place beyond the dyad also contribute to innovation.

The approach detailed in this book extends traditional perspectives on innovation that typically emphasize the final outcome that is usually viewed in isolation from the system within which it emerges. Therefore, the traditional perspectives that focus on innovation as an outcome are generally incomplete. These traditional studies of innovation are akin to studying an

J. D. Chandler, *Innovation, Social Networks, and Service Ecosystems*,
https://doi.org/10.1007/978-3-030-47797-4_2

elbow, without considering its role in connecting the forearms to the biceps and, more widely, its role in connecting the hand to the rest of the human body. Focusing solely on the elbow fails to capture the broader dynamics that help to clarify how and why an elbow functions as it does. In the same way, the traditional view of innovation that focuses only on a unique outcome, idea, or solution fails to capture the broader dynamics that help to clarify how and why unique and successful outcomes, ideas, or solutions function as they do. Considering the high-technology society in which we live, this would be similar to studying only a switch or processor chip without considering its role in the wider technological service ecosystem.

In order to better understand this embeddedness, it is useful to draw on philosophy and the idea of synergetics to generate a more holistic perspective on innovation. In this chapter, I propose a framework for thinking about how innovation emerges in a complex ecosystem. The main takeaway here is that systems are not rigid; they are dynamic and continuously evolving. Innovation is possible because ecosystems are always evolving. If an ecosystem will not or cannot evolve, then innovation is unlikely. Thus, it is important to be able to discuss the potential ability of systems to change.

To this end, I introduce the concept of plasticity, or the ability of a system to take and retain form. The plasticity, or resilience, of a system is important because the system must be able to evolve in order to survive disruption, which is the new norm in our digital economy. Because disruption has become the new norm, failure also needs to be a new norm. Failure takes many forms and looks like many different outcomes. Nevertheless, failure prepares systems for the changes that often occur with innovation. When the changes are too drastic, sometimes the system experiences shock. However, when the changes are not sufficiently divergent, they may be glossed over by the system. For this reason, failure plays an important but overlooked role in innovation. As mentioned in Chap. 1, innovation is a process that includes both failures and successes. Understandably, failure is not often the outcome or final destination. Rather, failure often serves as a process by which a problem can be reframed and better understood. Failure is a way to gain more information such that a different and new approach can lead to a different outcome, one that may be more aligned with the system or that may bring the system into closer alignment with the proposed innovation. In order for the outcome to come to fruition, the system itself needs to change or adapt. The outcome itself is not the only new element that should be in consideration. The entire service ecosystem needs to have been changed, or evolved, in order for an innovative outcome to be considered successful in the traditional sense of what we consider innovation. This holistic, comprehensive process in its entirety is innovation.

To better navigate innovation as an all-encompassing complex dynamic process, a keen understanding of plasticity is fundamental. Plasticity gives us a language to talk about when a service ecosystem is ripe for change. Sometimes service ecosystems are not yet ready to evolve. That is, sometimes a service ecosystem is perfectly functional, but it is not the appropriate time for a new idea or outcome. Without proper timing, an innovation may not prosper in a particular service ecosystem. The same innovation may prosper in one service ecosystem but not another. It is like picking a fruit from a tree; the fruit may be perfectly good; however, it just may not be the right time to harvest the fruit. The timing needs to be right, and various elements need to have been in place in order to have a successful harvest.

Because of the constant disruption that characterizes the digital economy and contemporary society, it is necessary to consider the timing inherent to managing and harnessing value. This is the purpose of this chapter. In the next section, I will first explain plasticity, followed by its four principles of recursivity, temporality, complementarity, and continuity. Following that section, I will then illustrate and explain synergetics. Finally, I will propose a deeper framework for appreciating how data, big data, machine learning, and artificial intelligence influence the service ecosystems in which they are embedded.

Plasticity

Because service ecosystems continuously evolve, it is important to understand plasticity—the ability of systems to adapt, take, and retake form (Alderson 1957; Nenonen et al. 2014). An ecosystem's plasticity depends on whether or not its systemic elements can converge or diverge synchronously as a cohesive system (Sterman 2000). If they can adapt in a synchronous way, then the system as a whole can thrive. If they cannot adapt synchronously, then the system may become disrupted or unstable.

To better explain this, I draw on philosophy and the idea of plasticity, or the systemic capacity of various systemic elements to receive form, give form, or annihilate all forms in a cohesive way. Based on this, plasticity is a systemic measure of its adaptability, or a measure of how well a system overall can thrive in the future. Although systems are continually changing, their plasticity gives an idea of whether evolution is well balanced, without too much instability or too much stability. If there is too much instability in a service ecosystem, it can be disrupted or destroyed easily. If there is too much stability in a service ecosystem, it is resistant to change.

Because of the many different social structures, ideas, and resources competing or converging in a service ecosystem, these various elements must be harmonized in order to establish and maintain a healthy level of plasticity (Kjellberg et al. 2015). Imagine masses of people, organizations, and governments that exist and operate without any order; without an overarching impetus that motivates mutually beneficial behaviors, the chaos that would ensue among these different groups and actors would damage all of the others in some way or form. On the other hand, when they operate in a way that is conducive for all of their successes to jointly occur, they operate as a system. Sometimes, the various elements do not need explicit coordination; this occurs when there is value for the entire system and all systemic actors benefit in some way when other systemic actors also individually succeed or benefit. On the other hand, when systemic actors and elements are not explicitly coordinated (or are implicitly coordinated), sometimes only some actors or elements in the system benefit, while others become damaged or wither away. In other words, only some actors gain value, while others gain less or no value. When there is value in the system, most actors and elements benefit from being connected to the system. Similarly, imagine technological devices and software codes that all exist and operate independently. Even though there are thousands and millions of such devices and codes, without an industry-wide protocol or a generational standard these collections of hardware and software would not be able to function interdependently as a cohesive system. From a technological perspective, the value is in the individual components functioning as a cohesive whole. Stated differently, value emerges from the components operating as a system.

Since value significantly shapes the individual behaviors of actors in a system, value implicitly coordinates the individual behaviors of the various actors or devices in a way that the actions of all are mutually beneficial to various other actors embedded in the same system. At the micro, meso, and macro levels, the properties, processes, and dynamics related to these individual actors often vary. Although the beneficial outcomes differ at the micro, meso, and macro levels, the properties, processes, and dynamics of the system integrate through and across each of these levels. But, because value is a systemic organizing principle, it is embedded in and cannot be separated from either the individual micro level (e.g., customer value) or the collective macro level (e.g., public value) (Prahalad and Ramaswamy 2004; Lusch and Vargo 2006). Plasticity emerges from the degree to which systemic elements are or can be harmonized, as well as the likelihood of maintaining this harmonization. Thus, each system can have a different level and nature of plasticity. Because each individual actor and element is unique, the combination of actors and elements in a particular system is unique. Thus, each system has "potentiality for being remolded and responding in a different way thereafter" (Alderson 1957, p. 277). Because of this, it is difficult to predict how systemic elements together will react to change. As a result, it is not easy to predict how value propositions might be evaluated and how innovation might occur in a service ecosystem.

Service ecosystems can differ from one another on multiple dimensions; for example, they may differ by high or low degrees of fluidity, or by high or low degrees of stability. Fluidity is the capacity of the service ecosystem to take on a different form or be molded, and stability is the capacity of the service ecosystem to retain a particular form or remain at a particular equilibrium (Nenonen et al. 2014). Fluidity and stability are interdependent dimensions of plasticity. They are not opposites. A service ecosystem can be high in both fluidity and stability, or low in both fluidity and stability. Also, a service ecosystem can be high on one dimension while being low in the other. Fluidity and stability together represent how service ecosystems respond to value creation efforts (Kjellberg et al. 2015).

If systemic elements all respond positively to a value proposition, there is wider systemic change and harmonization of innovation efforts. In a high-technology environment, consider that the value proposition could be a new software or a new data point. If this new software or data point generates positive reactions from other systemic elements, the system is more easily adaptable to the new software or data. If systemic elements all respond negatively to a value proposition, there is very little or no systemic change and innovation efforts are largely rejected. Continuing the previous example, if systemic elements respond negatively to a new software for new data, then the system will not change and innovation efforts are generally impeded. If the reaction of elements is mixed (some negative, some positive), there is some degree of systemic change. In high-technology environments, this is usually the case. Because the reactions of systemic elements to new software or new data are often mixed, customer service and technological support services can help to ameliorate the various responses. In this way, technical support staff have begun to play a role that is closely aligned with helping individuals in the system adapt to change. For example, in many mobile device applications, chat-bots serving as customer service support may collect data about different user interfaces or user environment challenges that are not yet accommodated by the mobile application. In real-time, these bots make programmers and developers aware of the flaws in the mobile application so that the software can be adapted to the user environment challenges, or value proposition. This encompasses a continuous revision of the software. In this way, the service ecosystem is always thriving, balancing change with some fluidity and some stability.

However, these incessant invitations that arrive in the forms of value propositions and the continuous introductions of innovation efforts do not necessarily occur as high magnitude events. Rather, the invitations might be narrow or small, and innovation may take the form of an individual actor simply voicing an opinion. Over time, these smaller behaviors may erode existing parameters that give order to an ecosystem. In this way, innovation is ongoing in a continuous process by which both small and large perturbations may influence the service ecosystem. Because systemic elements may interact differently, a different logic or order parameter may emerge as some form of innovation. As mentioned previously, innovation is a complex process that includes both failures and successes. There are many different states of equilibrium, fluidity, and stability for a particular service ecosystem. Over time, a service ecosystem may reach different degrees of each. Accordingly, these influence plasticity, which in turn influences the system's ability to evolve in response to a new value proposition or innovation effort (Van de Ven and Poole 1990).

In innovation research, the traditional investigation often explores the impact or incredibility of the innovation. However, the proposed perspective emphasizes plasticity, which centers on the systemic reception or response to innovation. Stated differently, plasticity is important because it represents the fertility of the soil that receives a seed of innovation. The number of invitations, or value propositions, helps to prepare the soil, or the service ecosystem, for the innovation. Although some of these may seem like failed value propositions, the effort may have prepared the system for innovation. Without the previous efforts, it is possible that the successful value proposition would not have thrived. In other words, the previous interactions may have improved the plasticity of the service ecosystem. On the other hand, if a service ecosystem is low in plasticity, then an innovation cannot flourish.

By understanding plasticity, it is possible to begin thinking holistically about the dimensions and traits of service ecosystems that can contribute to innovation and value creation. It is also important to note that service ecosystems exist on a temporal continuum and, as such, can have more plasticity at one point time and less plasticity at another point in time. Thus, plasticity is not a static variable. It can influence innovation in different ways, depending on the point in time at which the innovation and service ecosystem interact. Generally speaking, innovation is influenced by plasticity in four ways: recursivity, temporality, complementarity, and continuity. Each of these is described below.

Recursivity

Recursivity refers to the reaction of systemic elements to dissonance in the service ecosystem. This can include beliefs, emotions, cognitions, behaviors, and actions regarding potential value creation. When a value proposition is introduced to a service ecosystem, it is rare for all systemic elements to react uniformly. Some may react negatively, while others may react positively. Moreover, a systemic element may react to a value proposition as a threat or an opportunity. As a result, some systemic elements may either strengthen or weaken their reactions in order to remain harmonized with other systemic elements. At this point, the value proposition is merely a perturbation or disturbance to the service ecosystem. It has not yet become established as an order parameter and the system is attempting to self-adjust in response to it. The overall effect that it might have on the service ecosystem is not yet clear. Individual systemic elements adjust to provide greater fluidity and stability to the service ecosystem in a recursive way. This adjustment comprises a feedback loop that facilitates plasticity; the fluidity allows the service ecosystem to move toward taking on a new form, while the stability maintains synchronicity in the service ecosystem. It is not yet clear, at a systemic level, how the value proposition will be received.

Each systemic element reacts locally to the value proposition; in other words, each systemic element typically reacts in a way that optimizes its local position and situation. For instance, some systemic elements may interact with other elements in order to harmonize their response to the value proposition. This feedback loop can create a new path and introduce more stability to the service ecosystem. At the same time, to enhance service ecosystem fluidity, other systemic elements may disassociate with one another. In this feedback loop, a different order may emerge that elicits response from other systemic elements. Multiple disparate feedback loops in a service ecosystem disseminate throughout the system and catalyze clusters of change. Meanwhile, there is convergence around value propositions as they are introduced to the service ecosystem. Fluidity of the service ecosystem increases, and there is possible disruption of prevailing order parameters. In other words, the innovation process gains momentum.

The feedback loops that transpire during innovation are thus important for subsequent value propositions that are later introduced to the service ecosystem and are pivotal for moving the innovation process forward. Transformed beliefs or learned knowledge often emerge in response to value propositions, and these ultimately stimulate feedback loops. When habits, culture, or attitudes change in response to feedback loops, ideas and institutions also change during the innovation process. When systemic elements intermingle, they may influence one another and change the nature of the service ecosystem. The plasticity of a service ecosystem influences recursivity, or the number and magnitude of feedback loops.

Temporality

When a value proposition is introduced to a service ecosystem, it can also catalyze stability, or retain form. This is especially true for service ecosystems that are highly fluid and like to take new forms. A service ecosystem's plasticity influences the speed of systemic response once a value proposition has been introduced to a service ecosystem. In this way, plasticity influences a value proposition by the velocity of the response by systemic elements. When a value proposition is introduced to a service ecosystem, it may not always be well received. In most stable service ecosystems, existing patterns among systemic elements resonate with other existing patterns and together these are remembered throughout the service ecosystem. However, in service ecosystems that are less stable, the recursivity and feedback loops that occur in response to a value proposition may establish different values and behaviors that then reverberate through the service ecosystem. As innovation is pursued over time, the service ecosystem can change in nature. This can occur at either the micro, meso, or macro levels of the service ecosystem. When systemic elements at each of these levels become harmonized, the service ecosystem becomes more stable over time.

Complementarity

At first, a value proposition is introduced. Then some systemic elements initially react to the value proposition. Ultimately, the other systemic elements that were interconnect with the initial elements then also react to the value proposition and their changed relationship with other systemic elements. This increases the capacity of the service ecosystem to retain a new form by establishing different norms, rules, and beliefs in the service ecosystem. As a result, the service ecosystem is more stable than it was previously. Increasingly, there are shorter feedback loops that then increase alignment throughout the service ecosystem including synchronizing values, beliefs, and behaviors at the micro, meso, and macro levels. Although this synchronization is not explicit, the recursive feedback loops increase complementarity among systemic elements. Sometimes, the complementarity is fruitful and the innovation efforts are successful. At other times, the complementarity does not work and the innovation efforts fail since the systemic elements are not harmonized in their response to the value proposition. Plasticity of a service ecosystem influences the complementarity that can then influence the value proposition. A high degree of fluidity is needed to achieve complementarity so that individual systemic elements can more easily harmonize with the other elements.

Continuity

Although a value proposition has been introduced to the service ecosystem, it is possible that some systemic elements may not be calibrated adequately with others. This creates upheaval in the service ecosystem, which deteriorates into further disarray. Attempting to achieve a new or revised equilibrium, feedback loops catalyze different responses, perturbations, and processes. It is not immediately clear which of these will eventually dominate. It is also possible that extant processes may be refined in some way. As these various new value propositions emanate out from their points of origin, the service ecosystem is filled with many, many value propositions. They may catalyze innovation processes in different places in a recursive process that may continue until a successful outcome is achieved.

Thus, innovation is constant, and the plasticity of a service ecosystem influences how the fluidity and stability of a service ecosystem ebbs and flows in response to a continuous wave of value propositions. Innovation is a systemic process that never ends, never fails, and never truly succeeds—especially since a service ecosystem is always in flux. Innovation is the constant state of disruption that we have come to know in the digital economy. Innovation does not require a complete ending of the story, nor does it require full alignment of a service ecosystem (Baron et al. 2017). Ultimately, the continuity and the disruption of the digital economy are unlikely to fade so it is more helpful to harness their power than to wish them away.

When a value proposition is proposed in a service ecosystem, it often evolves in response to the many pressures of the service ecosystem (Ordanini et al. 2013; Skålén et al. 2015). Since service ecosystems cannot be controlled by a single actor, innovation also cannot be controlled by a single actor (Vargo et al. 2015; Koskela-Huotari et al. 2016; Siltaloppi et al. 2016). So, as a result, the value proposition that emerges as an innovation can sometimes look different, much like a unique and new idea that has been revised, revised, and revised again by elements in the service ecosystem as it gained wider acceptance (Adner and Kapoor 2010; Gawer and Cusumano 2013). Generally speaking, when existing solutions are insufficient for solving existing problems, service ecosystems begin to stop being self-organized. Departing from old-order parameters, systemic elements begin to vibrate differently and new ways of activity begin to emerge. Sometimes, there are inconsistencies when each level of the service ecosystem is viewed separately; for example, the micro-level individual behaviors may not coincide or harmonize with macro-level cultural values. As Kurtmollaiev and colleagues illustrate, these inconsistencies can begin to stimulate a change in systemic logic. Because the inconsistencies affect some elements more than others, only some systemic elements will react (Skålén et al. 2015; Fligstein and McAdam 2011).

Understanding innovation from this perspective clarifies that there are many starts and stops in the process, and that the process is complex and multifaceted. Innovation is not a stage-gate linear process, nor is it a messy design-thinking exercise in creativity. Rather, innovation is a series of trials and errors, failures and successes. These, together, prepare the service ecosystem for a new successful outcome for problems that are rather old. Innovation is the response to pressure, and the process by which we come to terms with our endeavors to find meaning and happiness. Like a circular change, the innovation pendulum swings back and forth balancing out the different forms and states of a service ecosystem. By showing innovation as an ongoing process, the networked and systemic nature of innovation is highlighted (Dhanaraj and Parkhe 2006; Clarysse et al. 2014; Zahra and Nambisan 2012). When innovation is viewed in this way, the role of the service ecosystem becomes clear: the service ecosystem is where a value proposition initiates how an innovation ultimately takes form and function. Viewing innovation as isolated from the service ecosystem does not fully capture how systemic elements might resist, adapt, or react to value propositions. Further, viewing innovation as isolated from the service ecosystem does not show the necessity of failures and feedback loops on the road to beneficial outcomes. Finally, and most important, viewing innovation as isolated from the service ecosystem does not demonstrate the implicit and explicit coordination and collaboration required to emerge potentially beneficial outcomes. Viewing innovation in isolation from the true innovation process is like looking at an incomplete picture without a background.

Synergetics

Because value informs how a system self-organizes, it informs how a system evolves in response to internal influences. Rather than emphasize external triggers or jolts, synergetics emphasizes internal systemic consistency. This is an extension of most studies of service ecosystems since these tend to be studied when they are changed by an external event. The emphasis of synergetics on the study of systems that are changed internally offers insights to how we think about innovation.

Many systems are self-organizing. Synergetics, based in the social sciences, articulates value as a simultaneously individual and collective phenomenon (von Hayek 1977; Meynhardt et al. 2016). Artificial intelligence and machine learning, for example, are designed to be self-organizing systems. The logic of the system is set by the individual behaviors captured in the data which ultimately train the system to behave according to a certain parameter. One reason why artificial intelligence and machine learning are so resilient is that they are internally determined. In other words, they do not need direction or attention from outside of the system in order to evolve.

As will be illustrated subsequently, self-organized systems are more difficult to disrupt than systems that are explicitly and externally coordinated. With respect to innovation, it would be difficult to introduce new ideas, or knowledge in self organized stable systems. In other words, in self-organized systems, it is difficult to change the progression of the systemic elements especially as they become more and more intertwined over time. Essentially, when systems become stable because there is sustainable change among the systemic elements, there is enslavement and often also consensualization; in these systems, the smaller parts and processes of the system complement one another and inform change (Meynhardt 2009). In machine learning and artificial intelligence service ecosystems, the smaller parts of the service ecosystem are the codes and data that are inserted into the system from outside the system. The data often reflect human behavior in the real world, which is typically repetitive and habitual. Based on this, machine learning and artificial intelligence service ecosystems are designed to generally continue into the future based upon these behavioral patterns. Furthermore, because of these patterns, the intent in most machine learning and artificial intelligence scenarios is to remove human interference from the machine learning process or the artificial intelligence process. Ultimately, the designer of the machine learning system or artificial intelligence system intends to remove human decision-making from the system such that the codes regenerate automatically based on data contained in the related data warehouses, and the system can behave autonomously.

Value creation is thus inherent within such systems, and, as a result, in such systems innovation is likely to be more difficult. This is because value is contextual since all the various parts and pieces of a service ecosystem contribute to it, and all of these are bound together seamlessly and cohesively because of it. For this reason, value creation is best understood with a broadened lens that extends beyond more than a single component or level of the service ecosystem. This lens is necessary because it makes each of the individual parts or levels of a service ecosystem salient and as holistic and mutually constitutive within the comprehensive whole. Similarly, the whole is a complex culmination of its parts and processes. In this way, the system and its elements are characterized by a mutual constitution that make it difficult to study value in the absence of these various system elements (Giddens 2016). Stated simply, value is unique—or contextual—to the service ecosystem in which it is embedded. Value is unique to the context in which it is embedded.

Heyde points attention to those smaller parts and processes that comprise the context surrounding value creation. He outlines how that which is "valuable" is valuable because of a relationship between an object and a subject (Meynhardt et al. 2016). To illustrate, consider that value creation requires an object and a subject to relate to, or value, the object. When value creation occurs, value organizes the subject's action or behavior toward the object, and vice versa. It is because of the action or behavior, and the relationship between the object and the subject, that value creation occurs. Furthermore, it is because of the relationship between the object and the subject that value exists. Because of these processes, value is forever attached to all of these and cannot exist on its own. When disruption occurs, the relationship between an object and subject may change. In turn, the relationship shift is what may dislodge value from being attached to the system.

Given this and as discussed in Chap. 1, value acts as an organizer of systems because it unifies and aligns the various actors and elements in a system. As the organizer, value manifests at different magnifications when researchers focus on particular actions, processes, and behaviors at micro, meso, or macro levels of a service ecosystem (Chandler and Vargo 2011). Because value is action-, process-, and behavior-oriented, value is salient in the change states, or transitions, of a service ecosystem. For this reason, it is necessary to move beyond a static network perspective to a dynamic systems perspective in order to view the transitions between and among states of a service ecosystem.

One way to begin thinking more clearly about change states is to conceptualize innovation as the ecosystem beginning and ending with a state of "emergence" and a state of "enslavement" surrounding value (Meynhardt et al. 2016). Drawing on the language of philosophy, synergetics asserts that value provides order to service ecosystems which would have otherwise existed in continuous chaos. Because value is a core organizing principle in service ecosystems, the actors engaged in service ecosystems respond to value as an order parameter. Value implicitly coordinates the state transitions between "emergence" and "enslavement." Assuming value exists in a system, innovation may not necessarily need to occur since the system is stable. When there is stability in a system, the smaller elements already contribute actively to value creation. As a result, when a system is stable and systemic elements are jointly and synchronously moving on a future trajectory, failure is less of an appealing option for the system as a whole. This would deter value propositions from being evaluated (and subsequently accepted or rejected) in the service ecosystem. Because of the constant disruption in the digital economy, however, the system itself may not fail or change, but it may become disrupted by external jolts or triggers.

To account for this, it is necessary to better understand the interactions among the elements in a service ecosystem and how they contribute to self-organization. These elements can stimulate bottom-up emergences or top-down enslavements, which are interrelated (Meynhardt 2009). In a bottom-up emergence, the various parts of a service ecosystem contribute to or evolve "emergences." Sometimes, interactions at the micro level can unpredictably coalesce as macro-level properties while also stimulating change in other micro-level elements. When this occurs, macro-level properties become order parameters that originated from those initial micro-level elements and interactions. Then, on the other hand, a top-down enslavement occurs when the emerged order parameter then "enslaves" the remaining systemic elements. Although these forces emerge in response to one another, they differ qualitatively in nature from the micro-level elements and interactions that gave rise to them. Moreover, the emergences and order parameters are not simply a sum of the micro-level elements and interactions that gave rise to them. This is the basis of self-organization in a service ecosystem. Each of the elements, interactions, emergences, and order parameters are individually unique, complex, and dynamic. Additionally, they are not simply polar opposites of the other. This is because of the circular or nonlinear interactions among systemic elements. It is difficult to predict how the elements and interactions will influence one another, especially when new emergences or order parameters also shape the ecosystem. It is important to note that it is the relationships among the elements—and the relationships among the relationships—that are of key importance.

In a self-organizing system, order parameters only change when a system is critically destabilized. This can occur when the system is disrupted by an outside force, or when the smaller elements no longer emerge a dominant order parameter (i.e., when there is divergence). Moreover, when order parameters change, the behaviors of systemic elements becomes largely unpredictable. At the wider macro level, various order parameters may compete and cause institutional dissonance. The various order parameters stabilize and destabilize one another simultaneously, while the system as a whole waivers among various states. This continuous state of disruption continues until a new equilibrium is eventually reached, which may take some time. In such fluctuations between states, there is a critical point when the system is open to influence and diversity in elements, behaviors, processes, and routines. For a moment, varying yet contrasting order parameters may coexist. It is only when a system reaches the coveted "tipping point" that a dominant order parameter can begin to again successfully enslave systemic elements according to some logic.

The shift in self organization is necessary to understand with respect to innovation. As stated in Chap. 1, innovation is a complex multifaceted process that includes both failure and success. When a self-organized system is stable, value creation is stable and it is likely that value propositions will be ignored or rejected by systemic elements. Innovation, in this scenario, is unlikely since new ideas, knowledge, or outcomes cannot outweigh systemwide stability and synchronous value creation. However, when a self-organized system is critically destabilized, the system becomes open to influence, which could arrive in the form of a value proposition. At this crucial point in time, each systemic element seeks survival on its own terms since it can no longer rely on the order parameter that was implicitly coordinating systemwide behaviors and value creation. During these crucial times, value propositions are likely to be more fully evaluated and given every consideration. During these crucial times, innovation processes are likely to be initiated, restarted, failed, rescinded, then restarted again—with the ultimate outcome of arriving at a successful beneficial outcome for the system.

Stated differently, at the micro level, when value creation occurs, systemic elements interact with one another. Sometimes, new systemic elements come to exist. Together, these various elements contribute to an emergence of an order parameter, which stabilizes the service ecosystem. When extant elements evolve or change, or when new elements come to existence or are introduced to the system, the service ecosystem may adjust to accommodate the new elements. Established practices or processes may cease to make sense for the system to thrive. As a result, there may be a change in the logic of the system, which becomes destabilized to a point that liberates systemic elements from the old system logic. Then the system stabilizes a new order through a nonlinear process of bottom-up emergence and top-down consensualisation ("enslavement").

In order to relate enslavement and consensualization to innovation, it is important to determine how service ecosystems emerge, change, or solidify according to nine systemic principles of value creation: critical distance, stability, amplification, internal determination, nonlinearity and feedback, phase transitions, symmetry breaking, limited predictability, and historical dependence (Meynhardt et al. 2016). Detailed specifically below, these principles help to clarify how the "multiple interrelated actors, processes and systems that together move through phases and cycles" in service ecosystems jointly evolve, especially with respect to innovation.

Systemic Principle of Value Creation 1: Critical Distance

When a system is not at equilibrium, self-organization often begins to occur. This is due to the absence of equilibrium, which leads to various systemic elements distancing themselves from the point at which they would otherwise be. As a result, existing system values, elements, behaviors, and processes become destabilized. There is a high potential for value creation, or for the creation of beneficial outcomes that did not exist previously. At this point, value propositions are likely to be evaluated and innovation processes can be stimulated. Conversely, when a service ecosystem is at equilibrium, systemic elements continue on their pre-determined paths leading to typical beneficial outcomes. During these times, value propositions are not likely to be considered and innovation processes will often fail. On the other hand, during disequilibrium, therefore, new modes of value creation become possible and value propositions have a greater likelihood of eliciting new logics or order parameters.

Systemic Principle of Value Creation 2: Stability

Stability in a service ecosystem renders systemic elements less adaptable and less resilient. This is because systemic elements become accustomed to particular rules, norms, and behaviors. Value creation is stable so long as the system remains intact. Over time, as these remain the same, systemic elements also tend to remain the same. As a result, in stable service ecosystems, disturbances, or perturbations—such as value propositions and innovation—largely go unnoticed and have little effect. Value creation is established. However, in unstable service ecosystems, disturbances or perturbations can generate ripple effects or even disrupt systemic elements completely. This is because systemic elements are more adaptable and resilient, which can lead to more opportunity for value creation. Over time, as rules, norms, and behaviors change and evolve, systemic elements also tend toward change. At these points, value propositions and innovation can be more fruitful, although they may also be too disruptive. Despite this, there is a fine balance between stability and instability for value creation. In completely unstable service ecosystems, disturbances or perturbations might be disruptive, while in service ecosystems with some degree of stability systemic elements may be more easily adaptable to change.

Systemic Principle of Value Creation 3: Amplification

Generally speaking, service ecosystems can be characterized by particular states of existence. Some may be salty, while some may be cold. Others may be productive, and others may be hostile. These states can waiver from “not at all” to “extreme” (e.g., a system range from either “not at all cold” to “extremely cold”). Changes in the characteristics of a service ecosystem coincide with changes to systemic elements. When state changes are drastically different or are polar opposites from the previous state, there is amplification. This is important for innovation because drastic state changes can signal either failure or success during an innovation process; it is important to be aware of system states, as well as systemic state changes.

Systemic Principle of Value Creation 4: Internal Determination

Emergences are often unexpected or unpredictable because they largely depend on internal order parameters. The dynamics that give rise to emergences are invisible, yet they are infallible. For this reason, when an service ecosystem is internally determined and stable, it is difficult to create value from the outside. Value propositions and innovation efforts are likely to be ignored. Rather, the dynamics and parameters of the service ecosystem should be observed and studied in order to evaluate upon the best options for value creation.

Systemic Principle of Value Creation 5: Nonlinearity and Feedback Loops

When a system is internally determined through self-organization, it relies upon the nonlinear dynamics that are typically characterized by feedback loops. Various systemic elements can together stimulate loops that exert influence back on themselves and other systemic elements. In this way, service systems are not entirely linear moving through time and space uniformly. Rather, service systems consist of some nonlinearity in that elements can react back in unique and often unpredictable ways. It is important to understand nonlinearity in order to offer value propositions and initiate innovation efforts that capitalize on feedback loops.

Systemic Principle of Value Creation 6: Phase Transitions

Systemwide changes in values, elements, behaviors, or processes are indicative of phase transitions, as a service ecosystem moves through time. Because service ecosystems are dynamic, continuous, and always changing, phase transitions are always happening. It is necessary to find the patterns among service ecosystems in order to delineate each phase transition. Value propositions and innovation efforts should be appropriate to the current phase transition of the service ecosystem.

Systemic Principle of Value Creation 7: Symmetry Breaking

When new order parameters establish new logics in service ecosystems, an emergence has come to fruition. This often destabilizes the system and moves away from the previous equilibrium. This is symmetry breaking. Over time, order parameters become established for service systems. When this occurs, it is difficult to begin offering compelling value propositions and even more difficult to bring innovation efforts to fruition since the system has just reached a new equilibrium.

Systemic Principle of Value Creation 8: Limited Predictability

Irregular, unpredictable processes are not typically predictable beyond the short term. It is unlikely to see the system beyond the immediate horizon. For this reason, it is difficult to plan for compelling value propositions too far in advance. It is even more difficult to execute long-term innovation efforts.

Systemic Principle of Value Creation 9: Historical Dependence

Every action, emergence, behavior, or process in a service system is the culmination of every previous action, emergence, behavior, or process. In the position of every element, information relevant for future actions can be derived from the current position of the element. This is because of historical dependence. Value propositions and innovation efforts should not be offered or initiated without appropriate consideration of the past.

The Influence of Big Data, Machine Learning, and Artificial Intelligence

The availability, capture, and storage of data influence how service ecosystems organize. Data are at the foundation of machine learning and artificial intelligence. When a system of machine learning or artificial intelligence organizes, the data act as order parameters, thereby informing the direction of system response to internal and external influences. The data establish a logic that is based on past behaviors, norms, beliefs, and attitudes such that external triggers or jolts do not deter the system. In this way, there is internal systemic consistency. The logic of the system is set by individual behaviors, beliefs, norms, and attitudes captured in the data. These datapoints emerge as certain order parameters. Because of this, a machine learning or artificial intelligence systems do not need direction or attention from outside the system in order to evolve. Moreover, this makes artificial intelligence and machine learning more resilient than systems that require constant outside attention. Because they are self-organized systems, artificial intelligence and machine learning systems are also difficult to disrupt. So, it is not within the system itself that innovation is likely to occur; rather, it is the application of such a system that is innovative. Artificial intelligence and machine learning systems would need to be embedded within a larger ecosystem to be most useful.

With respect to innovation, artificial intelligence and machine learning systems are unlikely to be sources of new ideas or knowledge unless those come in the form of simulations or projections into the future. Still, since these are self-organized stable systems, these simulations or projects would rely on status quo in order to be accurate. In other words, in artificial intelligence and machine learning systems, the interweaving of systemic elements becomes tighter over time since artificial intelligence and machine learning systems become more stable when there is both enslavement and consensualization. This is because the data together inform change in the future based upon past behavioral patterns. Ultimately, the designer of the machine learning system or artificial intelligence system intends to remove human decision-making from the system such that the codes regenerate automatically based on data contained in the related data warehouses, and the system can behave autonomously.

This is important for thinking about innovation because machine learning and artificial intelligence are based on stable data-driven systems. Once the data are established, the patterns, habits, and routines emerge into the order parameters that influence machine learning and artificial intelligence. Unless an external influence (such as a code or programmer) infuses an externally determined parameter, machine learning and artificial intelligence will be based on the data derived from past patterns, habits, and routines. Value creation is thus inherent in such systems. Value is contextual and unique to each system since the various parts and pieces of each service ecosystem contribute to value. As a result, they are all bound together seamlessly and cohesively because of value. For this reason, value creation is best understood with a broadened lens that extends beyond more than a single component or level of the service ecosystem. In artificial intelligence and machine learning systems, each of the individual parts or levels are mutually constitutive within the comprehensive whole. The entire service ecosystem is a complex culmination of its smaller parts and processes. This mutual constitution makes it difficult for innovation to occur within the parameters of service ecosystem itself.

Because value dynamically organizes a service ecosystem in this way, new value propositions are unlikely to destabilize artificial intelligence and machine learning systems. In these systems, the dynamics of "emergence" and "enslavement" are internally determined. Without these dynamics, artificial intelligence and machine learning systems would exist in continuous chaos. Because value is a core organizing principle in service ecosystems, artificial intelligence and machine learning systems are stable and the smaller elements are contributing actively to value creation. Artificial intelligence and machine learning systems themselves may not fail, although they could possibly be disrupted.

In artificial intelligence and machine learning systems, order parameters only change when a system is critically destabilized. This can occur when the system is disrupted by an outside force, or when data no longer emerge a dominant order parameter (i.e., when there is divergence). When order parameters change, artificial intelligence and machine learning systems become largely unpredictable. The various order parameters stabilize and destabilize one another simultaneously, while the system as a whole waivers among various states. This continuous state of disruption continues until a new equilibrium is eventually reached, which may take some time. In such fluctuations between states, there is a critical point when the system is open to influence and diversity in elements, behaviors, processes, and routines. In order to disrupt a stable system, it is necessary to insert a value proposition during one of these critical points.

Scholarly Takeaway

Service ecosystems waiver incessantly between stability and instability. Moreover, one of these is not necessarily better than the other because the characteristics of a service ecosystem accommodate different value propositions and value creation during stable states and unstable states. Generally speaking, stable service ecosystems are characterized by self-organization and internal dynamics. When service ecosystems are stable, it is difficult to introduce value propositions or innovation efforts to the systemic elements in these service ecosystems. However when service ecosystems are unstable, these service ecosystems are characterized by dissonance between and among systemic elements. Because there is less synchronicity among the various systemic elements, the service ecosystem is typically more adaptable to value propositions and innovation efforts. In other words, it is easier to introduce value propositions or innovation efforts to the systemic elements in these service ecosystems. In order to manage and harness value in the digital economy, it is necessary to be able to identify the states of service ecosystems. Based on this, it is then helpful to use the principles of systemic value creation as well as the concept of plasticity to better understand the nature of the service ecosystem and the place of a service ecosystem in its trajectory. By doing so, it is possible to gain a better understanding of the characteristics and timing that can make value propositions more compelling across different service ecosystems.

Managerial and Practical Takeaways

From a managerial perspective, the takeaway from this chapter is that service ecosystems are constantly changing and evolving in response to both internal and external factors. Artificial intelligence and machine learning are attempts to make service ecosystems more stable and resilient, by setting them up for autonomous self-organization. In this way the hope is that the service ecosystem can more easily continue into the future with very little human intervention. On a more general level, however, service ecosystems should be studied closely before attempting to offer value propositions so that the value propositions can become compelling enough to engage the appropriate actors for innovation. This in and of itself is not rocket science; however, it does require a good degree of observation and patience. It is necessary to understand the dynamics of a service ecosystem in order to be successful in the digital economy.

References

Adner, Ron, and Rahul Kapoor. 2010. Value Creation in Innovation Ecosystems: How the Structure of Technological Interdependence Affects Firm Performance in New Technology Generations. *Strategic Management Journal* 31 (3): 306–333. https://doi.org/10.1002/smj.821.

Alderson, Wroe. 1957. *Marketing Behavior and Executive Action: a Functionalist Approach to Marketing Theory*. Homewood: Richard Irwin.

Baron, Steve, et al. 2017. Feed People First. *Journal of Service Research* 21 (1): 135–150. https://doi.org/10.1177/1094670517738372.

Chandler, Jennifer D., and Stephen L. Vargo. 2011. Contextualization and Value-in-Context: How Context Frames Exchange. *Marketing Theory* 11 (1): 35–49. https://doi.org/10.1177/1470593110393713.

Chandler, Jennifer D., et al. 2018. How Does Innovation Emerge in a Service Ecosystem? *Journal of Service Research* 22 (1): 75–89. https://doi.org/10.1177/1094670518797479.

Clarysse, Bart, et al. 2014. Creating Value in Ecosystems: Crossing the Chasm Between Knowledge and Business Ecosystems. *Research Policy* 43 (7): 1164–1176. https://doi.org/10.1016/j.respol.2014.04.014.

Dhanaraj, Charles, and Arvind Parkhe. 2006. Orchestrating Innovation Networks. *Academy of Management Review* 31 (3): 659–669. https://doi.org/10.5465/amr.2006.21318923.

Fligstein, Neil, and Doug Mcadam. 2011. Toward a General Theory of Strategic Action Fields. *Sociological Theory* 29 (1): 1–26. https://doi.org/10.1111/j.1467-9558.2010.01385.x.

Gawer, Annabelle, and Michael A. Cusumano. 2013. Industry Platforms and Ecosystem Innovation. *Journal of Product Innovation Management* 31 (3): 417–433. https://doi.org/10.1111/jpim.12105.

Giddens, Anthony. 2016. *The Constitution of Society: Outline of the Theory of Structuration*. Cambridge: Polity.

Kjellberg, Hans, et al. 2015. Market Innovation Processes: Balancing Stability and Change. *Industrial Marketing Management* 44: 4–12. https://doi.org/10.1016/j.indmarman.2014.10.002.

Koskela-Huotari, Kaisa, et al. 2016. Innovation in Service Ecosystems – Breaking, Making, and Maintaining Institutionalized Rules of Resource Integration. *Journal of Business Research* 69 (8): 2964–2971. https://doi.org/10.1016/j.jbusres.2016.02.029.

Lusch, Robert F., and Stephen L. Vargo. 2006. Service-Dominant Logic: Reactions, Reflections and Refinements. *Marketing Theory* 6 (3): 281–288. https://doi.org/10.1177/1470593106066781.

Meynhardt, Timo. 2009. Public Value Inside: What Is Public Value Creation? *International Journal of Public Administration* 32 (3–4): 192–219. https://doi.org/10.1080/01900690902732632.

Meynhardt, Timo, Jennifer D. Chandler, and Pepe Strathoff. 2016. Systemic Principles of Value Co-creation: Synergetics of Value and Service Ecosystems. *Journal of Business Research* 69 (8): 2981–2989.

Nenonen, Suvi, et al. 2014. A New Perspective on Market Dynamics. *Marketing Theory* 14 (3): 269–289. https://doi.org/10.1177/1470593114534342.

Ordanini, Andrea, et al. 2013. When the Recipe Is More Important Than the Ingredients. *Journal of Service Research* 17 (2): 134–149. https://doi.org/10.1177/1094670513513337.

Patrício, Lia, et al. 2017. Upframing Service Design and Innovation for Research Impact. *Journal of Service Research* 21 (1): 3–16. https://doi.org/10.1177/1094670517746780.

Prahalad, C.K., and Venkat Ramaswamy. 2004. Co-creation Experiences: The Next Practice in Value Creation. *Journal of Interactive Marketing* 18 (3): 5–14. https://doi.org/10.1002/dir.20015.

Siltaloppi, Jaakko, et al. 2016. Institutional Complexity as a Driver for Innovation in Service Ecosystems. *Service Science* 8 (3): 333–343. https://doi.org/10.1287/serv.2016.0151.

Skålén, Per, et al. 2015. Cocreating the Arab Spring. *Journal of Service Research* 18 (3): 250–264. https://doi.org/10.1177/1094670514559700.

Sterman, John. 2000. *Business Dynamics: Systems Thinking and Modeling for a Complex World*. Boston: Irwin/McGraw-Hill.

Van De Ven, Andrew H., and Marshall Scott Poole. 1990. Methods for Studying Innovation Development in the Minnesota Innovation Research Program. *Organization Science* 1 (3): 313–335. https://doi.org/10.1287/orsc.1.3.313.

Vargo, Stephen L., et al. 2015. Innovation Through Institutionalization: A Service Ecosystems Perspective. *Industrial Marketing Management* 44: 63–72. https://doi.org/10.1016/j.indmarman.2014.10.008.

von Hayek, Friedrich A. 1977. *The Use of Knowledge in Society*. Menlo Park: Institute for Humane Studies.

Zahra, Shaker A., and Satish Nambisan. 2012. Entrepreneurship and Strategic Thinking in Business Ecosystems. *Business Horizons* 55 (3): 219–229. https://doi.org/10.1016/j.bushor.2011.12.004.

CHAPTER 3

The Micro and the Individual Innovator

The purpose of this chapter is to explore the nuances of innovation as it occurs at the individual micro level. This includes exploring what innovation looks like at the micro level, as well as describing and focusing on individuals as innovators. Traits of great innovators are also discussed.

Individual innovators are looking to solve problems in their own unique contexts. When service ecosystems waiver between stability and instability, it is because individual actors are attempting to solve problems in their own unique contexts. When different value propositions are offered, individual actors shape ecosystems by evaluating, accepting, or rejecting the value propositions. By doing so, they can potentially change the characteristics of a service ecosystem as they work to accommodate a value proposition within their own context. At the micro level, this is what value creation looks like as systems swing back and forth from stable states to unstable states.

Generally speaking, stable service ecosystems are characterized by self-organization and internal dynamics. At the individual innovator level, this means that value propositions are being introduced, evaluated, accepted, and rejected. When value propositions are adapted within service ecosystems that are stable, they are met with resistance and innovation efforts are difficult. However when value propositions are introduced to unstable service ecosystems, they are given more consideration because there is no guarantee that the existing dissonance between and among systemic elements will be resolved or address. When there is less synchronicity among

J. D. Chandler, *Innovation, Social Networks, and Service Ecosystems*,
https://doi.org/10.1007/978-3-030-47797-4_3

systemic elements, individual actors are more open to value propositions and innovation efforts.

Thus, individual innovators play a very important role in service ecosystems that are constantly changing. Although artificial intelligence and machine learning are attempts to make service ecosystems more stable and resilient, individual innovators are still needed to apply these systems where they are needed, especially because artificial intelligence and machine learning ecosystems can more easily continue into the future with very little human intervention. In many ways, artificial intelligence and machine learning ecosystems should serve to free humans from routine decision-making. This, in theory, should allow humans to act more mindfully and creatively about solving problems that they face in the particular service ecosystems in which they are embedded.

To this end, many believe that great innovators see spaces, places, and things that did not exist before. Innovators are painted as people who are thought to see beyond reality. Some believe that innovators live in two different worlds, with one foot planted firmly in the real world and the other foot floating in pure imagination. The greatest innovators of our time are supposed to be thinkers who do not merely listen, but think critically about what they perceive. They are thought to be intuitive and intense. They are viewed as humans who invent new things by foreseeing what others need or desire before those needs and desires are even recognized by others.

The most innovative companies, such as Google or Apple, are known worldwide for dominating their respective market spaces with unique, cutting-edge products and services that are difficult to imitate. When we think about the big minds at Google and Apple, innovation seems larger than life, almost beyond human. It seems that innovation at its finest is captured mostly in Silicon Valley, especially by the highly coveted high-tech technology companies that are changing the world. Based on this, some of the most innovative companies in the world think about innovation as taking or creating a vision of a particular future, and using that vision to guide their attempts to commercialize new products or services. In the most provocative discussion of innovation, innovators are discussed as everyday problem-solvers, rather than big thinkers.

However, the reality of innovation is much more mundane than that pictured in any of the perspectives above. Innovation often involves an everyday person with an everyday outlook coping with or attempting to address everyday problems. These everyday people innovate simply by being open to new ideas, or new value propositions. As a result, they often positively influence others around them, as well as other small privately held companies across different types of industries as well. These everyday humans often possess an innovation mindset to think about solving problems as they exist across many different types of industries, even at small companies, schools, universities, governments, and anywhere where problems hold us back from our finest moments.

No matter where we work or the challenges we face, our ability to innovate is what can drive our global competitiveness. To be innovators, we should always be mindful of existing trends and new emergent technologies. We need to think about issues in fields that are not always as exciting as high technology, like transforming manufacturing to be more sustainable or lessening equity gaps in education. We need to think about leading in our fields by seeking out excellence in all that we do so that we develop our own abilities to move forward and help others move forward as well. By improving ourselves, we transform business, government, and all kinds of organizations. And when this happens, we can innovate our economy.

The constant state of disruption that we face in the digital economy has given us an opportunity to develop leaders who embrace innovation as a complex nonlinear process. Because of instability and change in our service ecosystems, the time is ripe to inject value propositions and innovation efforts in order to reap beneficial outcomes for all those involved. This means changing the measures by which we assess our own success. Rather than focusing narrowly on revenue and profit, it is a good time to think about measures of corporate social responsibility, ethics, diversity, grit, and innovation, to name a few. As mentioned in Chaps. 1 and 2, the innovation process includes failure and also success. This means that in order to succeed at innovation, one must choose to fail at least initially. At the micro level, this means cultivating values such as such as courage and resilience in the face of adversity. In other words, innovation at the micro level looks like individuals being resilient.

Innovators are brave. They are comfortable with breaking through social norms. They are comfortable questioning conventional wisdom and are not afraid to think outside the box. Innovators are humble. They agree to put in the hard work and are persistent in working toward a solution without obtaining much recognition or reward. Nothing is too menial or too foolish to be given full consideration. Innovators embrace change. Innovators welcome different perspectives, fresh outlooks, and new ways of doing things. They are comfortable trying new activities and doing old things in ways that weren't done before. They look for environments where it is okay to challenge the status quo and to learn more. Innovators understand the importance of giving employees resources and tools to think more critically, so that they too can feel more empowered. Innovators have a healthy self-esteem. They don't seek to keep up with the Joneses or to put up with silly façades. They are concerned with continuous personal improvement and with making breakthroughs that are relevant to their personal lives. Innovators are value-oriented. They are mindful and conscientious. They are looking for commitment and highly productive people to work with. They need to feel valued and respected for living value-centered lives. And they need space to experiment, learn, and grow. Innovators are global citizens. They understand that meeting new people and talking about worldwide events and issues are sources of creativity. They build and sustain wide networks of acquaintances. They view collaboration as an opportunity. They understand that solutions don't magically appear in isolation, confiscated in a vacuum from the rest of the world. Innovators are open-minded. They understand that different viewpoints and different experiences help to develop a more comprehensive view of problems and solutions. They welcome diversity. Innovators can let go. They do not need to control outcomes. They develop trust with others on their teams and lead by example. They surround themselves with smart people, empower them, and then get out of the way. Innovators are persistent. They know that innovation doesn't happen overnight. They know that they need to navigate through resistance in order to build consensus. They know that status quo is difficult to challenge.

Among organizational leaders, a common concern is how to generate more innovation in their organization. Many managers look for innovators, or innovative people, who can spark new ideas and be creative. However, innovation is often prompted by a problem that is not going away. Instead of looking for people who tout solutions, it is important to look for people who can persistently attack a problem from all directions (Satell 2018). It is also important to build an organization's capacity for innovation by cultivating behaviors that empower others to also become more innovative. This leads to an organizational culture that centers on innovation. This is discussed in the subsequent chapters.

Trust, Advice, and Innovation

At a micro-level magnification of context or service ecosystems, individual actors are seen to be reaching out to one another directly. That is, each actor directly serves another actor. Together, the actors and the relationship that ensues between them is called a dyad. Dyads are important because both actors are active participants. In order to build an organization that can continuously innovate, it is necessary to focus on empowering individuals to solve the problems that they observe within their own contexts. This necessitates building a culture of trust so that individuals will be more comfortable reaching out to one another (Grant 1996; Van De Ven and Poole 1990; Zheng et al. 2010). Trust enables individuals to think more broadly about the problems they encounter in their contexts. When two individuals work collaboratively together within a dyad, they are also more honest with one another and take bigger risks when trying to solve existing problems since they can rely on one another. Because of the relationships that individuals have with others, trust helps individuals to rely on the actions of others that can help them to address problems.

As discussed in Chap. 2, innovation is typically discussed as an outcome by or of an individual person, an individual project team, or an individual organization (Yuan and Woodman 2010). However, a nonlinear, processual perspective of innovation emphasizes Paruchuri's perspective of innovation as "recombining and/or reconfiguring existing pieces of knowledge in some novel way" (p. 64). When focusing on the micro level, individual actors are seen as members of multiple dyads. In other words, each individual actor may reach out to and establish relationships with other individual actors. This helps each actor to gain access to different pieces of knowledge or information; for this reason, it is necessary for individuals who seek innovation to have access to a broad network of ideas. When there is trust, dyadic relationships strengthen the networks that can help individuals to recombine or reconfigure knowledge and information through engagement and dialogue with others. This important work that promotes innovation is done at the micro level. When an individual speaks to one another about an idea, the dialogue that ensues can potentially change the network and system. When the idea spreads throughout the network or system, it is because individual actors have engaged with others and dialogued with them. The work of innovation is rarely accomplished through policy changes or high-level management initiatives alone. Consequently, individual actors often play important roles in bridging among disparate groups in boundary spanning efforts to combine or reconfigure new ideas and information (Bryant 2005; Fleming et al. 2007; Powell et al. 1996). This perspective emphasizes innovation as it occurs outside of individuals, in dyads as individuals connect to one another and form relationships to address the problems that surround them.

Beyond trust, it is also important to cultivate social norms, rules, and beliefs that support problem-solving within these dyads so that new ideas can emerge and prosper (Chandler et al. 2018). This could involve, for example, breaking down silos in an organization so that individuals take ownership of projects, rather than focusing narrowly on the tasks that are assigned to them. In order to promote innovation, individuals must believe that the organization can change and adapt to new ideas or new value propositions. And finally, it is important to prioritize empathy such that active listening and brainstorming our central behaviors to the organization.

Innovation at the micro level involves individuals, as part of their problem-solving, reaching out to those around them. This being said, offering advice is also helpful for prompting innovation in the organization because advice-giving encourages collaborative learning. Moreover, advice-giving reifies the dyad relationship between two individuals. Because of advice-giving, the interpersonal skills and trust building required to move toward innovation are honed. Advice-giving can help individuals to think in new and different ways by overcoming framing effects on specific problems. Innovation often involves reframing a problem in a way that the problem can be addressed. When individuals become aligned within a dyad, the budding relationship offers informal mechanisms for advice-givers to offer new or alternative perspectives or access to organizational resources that can be helpful in specific situations.

It is important for trust and advice-giving to be prevalent throughout an organization that seeks to promote innovation. Trust and advice-giving allow different individuals to feel comfortable engaging in behaviors that offer others new ways to participate in the service ecosystem. To encourage behaviors related to innovation, managers can identify helpful, knowledgeable individuals and personally communicate with them on a one-on-one basis to encourage them to share their wisdom with others. Creating mentoring programs can also cultivate an organizational culture around these behaviors and also promote psychological safety. Again, these behaviors help to solidify dyadic relationships in the service ecosystem. It is also possible to encourage relationship building outside the traditional work day, in the evenings after work, at retreats, or on weekends. Individuals should be given ample time, opportunity, and space to interact both casually and formally in order to form both strong and weak dyadic relationships. For example, just before or after formal meetings, it can be helpful to provide opportunity for informal social interaction. This simple behavior can cultivate innovation by building trust and advice-giving behaviors among "weak" social ties where individuals are loosely affiliated without being close friends. Informal interactions are thus important for cultivating innovation because they shape the beliefs, values, orientations, behaviors, and skills and so on that facilitate innovation. They can be encouraging for individuals who need to seek advice, or who want to deliberate information with others. They help individuals to meet others with diverse opinions, attitudes, or judgments that may be different from their own. Although individuals may differ in opinions, attitudes, or judgments, it is important that a dialogue ensue among them in order create loosely affiliated dyads. The challenge of working with others on many different teams requires innovators to update their social norms, depart from old norms and adapt how they interact with new people. Dyadic relationships can help individual actors make these transitions by helping to build knowledge. Knowledge-sharing is often challenging when individuals are, at least initially, unfamiliar with one another.

Innovators are always looking for new knowledge generated from specific projects. In micro-level dyadic interactions, they learn from others who may also be working on the project. Since projects are often comprised of team members who are heterogeneous in knowledge, skills, and abilities, team members can learn from one another throughout the duration of the project. Again, trust and advice-giving help dyads to form in these situations. Oftentimes, social interactions are not directly related to the project, yet they can influence decision-making accuracy, especially when it comes to garnering task-related information. Individuals pursuing innovation typically require assistance with departing from old norms, or noticing and interpreting environmental. As individuals interact with one another for a longer period of time, trust grows and positively influences how they share knowledge. In turn, knowledge sharing across the organization is enhanced. Trust makes it typically easier to brainstorm and discuss new ideas.

This being said, friendship in the workplace is extremely important. Typically a voluntary and informal relationship, friendship is a dyadic relationship that is comprised of commitment, positive affect, accountability, and instrumentality. Friendships also cultivate the trust in dyads that make it easier to share and discuss new knowledge because there is also reciprocity. When friendships flourish, there is a higher level of reciprocity, commitment, trust, and positive affect throughout the organization, which cultivates open collaboration and the recombination of knowledge in new ways. This is because complex knowledge requires a higher level of codification and close ties, such as friendship, make it easier to share knowledge that is complex in nature.

Despite this, innovators should refrain from discussions about explicit knowledge, including declarative knowledge about facts that are specific and exact. These types of discussion are not especially fruitful for innovation because they do not require high levels of codification since the information is easy to articulate. Relationships built on these types of exchanges do not typically lead to innovation. Rather, it would be better for individuals seeking to be more innovative to look for explicit knowledge from websites or manuals. To expedite the transfer of explicit knowledge, it may be helpful to post and display on internal websites or to encourage social chatting applications so that individuals are not overwhelmed with requests for explicit knowledge.

Shared Language and Innovation

When learning about new ideas, information typically flows in an asymmetric, one-way direction from organizations to individuals. Generally speaking, organizations tend to dominate communications when it comes to new ideas. They do this through broadcast television advertising, social media, print advertisements and many other mainstream ways of putting out messaging. Recently, however, there has been more research about network effects that occur when new ideas are introduced to a population. The network effects are based on large groups of people who are initially exposed to the new idea, develop an evaluation of the idea, and then diffuse their evaluations through their social networks. In this day of high technology, much of these communications are happening on social media. Knowing this, many organizations have been smart about involving individuals in open feedback forms on their websites. Additionally, many organizations are tracking individuals as they visit their websites. Data collected about how long individuals might linger on that particular page, which keywords individuals might use and searching for new products, and where individuals are learning about the new products. These data are easily available on the Internet.

Individuals also help each other learn about new products from various forum such as Reddit, Twitter, and online game chat applications. Many video games, for example, are not sold with instruction manuals, yet individuals help each other to learn how to play video games by playing the same game on the same platform while chatting with one another using headsets. Because many of these video games offer many new features and capabilities, individuals work together to learn how to play the video games and help each other learn about defeating the enemy is on these games. Again, the friendship and trust help individuals to share new ideas.

Similarly, when new ideas or products or introduced to the market, individuals can be influenced by one another. Although they can indeed rely on organizational communications from advertising or from corporate websites, individuals seem to trust word-of-mouth evaluations particularly when these come from close friends and family members. Individuals are easily influenced by attitudes and decisions of their friends. Individuals pay close attention to the perceptions, wants, and desires of those who are in their closest social networks. Word of mouth spreads even faster now due to mobile devices and the World Wide Web. As a result, it is important to consider the conversation that is ongoing via social media.

Social media is an "online means of communication, conveyance, collaboration, and cultivation among interconnected and interdependent networks of people, communities, and organizations enhanced by technological capabilities and mobility". Social media is often user-generated content that is shared on platforms by all users with the intent of sharing it with all other users. Because of social media, individuals can send out information, acquire information, and talk about new ideas with people from all over the world. This has stimulated an openness such that information is no longer standardized in a one-size-fits-all message. Social media has played a fundamental and large role in this transformation because it has allowed individuals to become active co-creators of content.

Social media also plays an important role in innovation because social media overall increases trust and communication across society. Tuten and Solomon suggest that social media can play different functions in society. For example, social media helps to build community; this happens on social media channels that are encouraging interpersonal relationships and facilitating common interests among individuals. This is important for innovation because stronger interpersonal relationships build trust and help to cultivate the openness required for innovation. As described previously, social media is also important for content distribution and for organizational communications. Social media is also a basis for enjoyment and entertainment, including, for example, video games and streaming music or online content.

When it comes to building social community on social media, individuals can communicate with one another and share experiences, collaborate, and bond with others. This is important for innovation because members of a community come to share language and mental models. When a community begins to have a common language, it is a sign that the community shares perceptions of the world around them and see the world similarly. This suggests that problem framing can be more effective when a community emerges among those who perceive the existence of a problem. When different people see a problem in the same way, it is easier for them to work together toward a solution; additionally, there is some consensus around potential solutions. This makes it easier to innovate.

Plasticity at the Micro Level

With respect to plasticity as described in Chap. 2, individual innovators play a significant role in how a service ecosystem adapts to value propositions and innovation efforts. To begin with, individual innovators influence recursivity by often being the ones who stimulate the feedback loops that lead to change among systemic elements. This can increase fluidity in a service ecosystem by allowing the service ecosystem to take new forms. This is because innovators are often bridge spanners, thereby connecting individuals in different subgroups regarding value propositions or innovation efforts. Moreover, innovators tend to associate with diverse sets of individuals who can bring different ideas to different parts of the service ecosystem. This again positively influences fluidity in the service ecosystem.

Individual innovators can also affect the temporality of plasticity by speeding or slowing the responses of the service ecosystem to value propositions or innovation efforts. For example, if there are more innovators in a particular service ecosystem, then the responses to a value proposition or innovation effort are likely to be faster because innovators are typically open to new ideas and change. On the other hand, if there are fewer innovators in a service ecosystem, then the responses to value propositions or innovation efforts are likely to be slower since those who do not have an innovation mindset will likely resist change and new ideas. Similarly, in service ecosystems characterized by high numbers of innovators, it is likely that systemic elements will react more in ways that are more complementary to the value propositions and innovation efforts; in other words, the service ecosystem will revert back to synchronicity more quickly. Conversely, for service ecosystems that are characterized by low numbers of innovators, it is likely that systemic elements will not react as positively with respect to new value propositions or innovation efforts and the service ecosystem will either be slow to realign or will not realign at all. Finally, because of the persistence of innovators, service ecosystems will likely thrive and continuously evolve. However, service ecosystems characterized with high numbers of innovators are likely to reach this phase faster and with less effort, while service ecosystems characterized with low numbers of innovators are likely to stall in their evolution toward reaching synchronicity.

Ironically, when managers need to stabilize their service ecosystems, they should be aware and conscientious about individuals who demonstrate the traits of innovators. Although innovators are open to change and new ways of thinking, innovators are likely to be seen as "rocking the boat" which is considered to destabilize the service ecosystem. Too much change too quickly is likely to jolt the service ecosystem. Conversely stated, if managers need to open up their service ecosystems in order to make them more resilient or prepare them for change, they should encourage behaviors related to innovation. They should encourage informal dialogue and interaction, risk-taking, and a diverse set of viewpoints.

Rise of the "T" Professional

Given the complexity of innovation, there is a growing and urgent need for "T" professionals who can speak and operate across disciplinary boundaries by drawing on skills and knowledge from various streams of research in order to develop their own depth in a particular area. They are systems thinkers and adaptive innovators. Instead of searching for "random" innovators, managers need to pursue service science and "T" professionals that are trained and nested in innovation.

The idea of a T professional was first described by David Guest in 1991. It is the idea that individuals should develop their knowledge bases and skill sets in the shape of a “T”. “T” professionals have a deep knowledge base and skill set in one specific area, but can complement that specificity with a wider knowledge base and broader skill set across many different areas.

These professionals are inquisitive and are willing to try new things. They are curious about the world and are empathetic to the people with whom they work, which stimulates their own exploration of perspectives other than their own. They recognize how different approaches contribute to their understanding of the problem from a high-level humanistic perspective. In this way, they can integrate different knowledge bases and skill sets to complement their primary knowledge base and skill set.

A key trait of tea professionals is empathy. This empathy is important because it creates a culture on the team where team members are likely to build on one another’s ideas. Empathy is important because it helps individuals to see problems from the perspectives of the others on the team. Rather than shutting down and forcing others to acquiesce to their own perspectives, T-shaped professionals are open to seeing the world from different perspectives. Some behaviors that reflect empathy and are helpful in the workplace include active listening and asking questions.

Traditional higher education creates graduates who tend to have deep and specific knowledge bases and skill sets. This is not ideal because these individuals tend to see problems from only one perspective. As a result, the solution sets that they are willing to consider are limited and generally oriented toward solutions from their educational backgrounds. Also they tend to be less open to other ways of thinking when they are working on teams in the workplace.

T-shaped professionals however understand systems, which is important for understanding major services such as healthcare, education, or energy for example. These large-scale service ecosystems are comprised of various types of factors, including people, technology, hardware systems, ecological systems, and so on. T-shaped professionals understand how such service ecosystems function with respect to impacting quality of life. T-shaped professionals also are aware that they need to be adaptive and are willing to work across disciplines. For engineer, for example, the vertical bar of the T can include technical fundamentals related to software coding or structural engineering, while the horizontal bar of the T can include an awareness of business functional areas and societal values as based in sociology.

In response to the continuous state of disruption brought about by the digital economy, it is important for organizations to be quick to respond to new value propositions and innovation efforts. Organizations should always be looking for agile ways to work. They should also encourage cross-functionality on teams that are comprised of professionals with deep knowledge bases and skill sets in different areas. This is difficult to achieve because organizations are typically built around functional areas, in which individuals possess and develop similar skill sets. Traditionally, individuals built their entire careers honing their specialties in becoming experts in their area. Typically, as they gain and demonstrate expertise in a specific skill set, their value also increases to the organization. This approach has also made it easier for the organization to develop competencies in a specific area.

However, it is necessary to develop the cross-functionality needed on organizational teams in order to address the constant state of disruption that characterizes today's digital economy. This is necessary because it is difficult to move large projects from one large functional area of the organization to another large functional area. The coordination costs are high and project managers find it difficult to cross these organizational boundaries. It is difficult for project managers to communicate in the "different languages" needed for each functional area. Moreover, when projects move from one functional area of the organization to another, knowledge is lost and decisions that were made are often lost in translation. The functional areas become highly siloed and individuals in each area fail to see the project in its larger context. They only see their tasks, and are held accountable only for completing their own tasks. Many individuals defer problem-solving to others since they are only responsible for their own narrow components of the project. This contributes to the lack of motivation to expand knowledge bases and skill sets.

One way to overcome this challenge is to cultivate teams that are T shaped. In T-shaped teams, each team member has a different set of expertise, knowledge, and skills. As the individuals work together on teams, they acquire different knowledge bases and skill sets. The team overall becomes more versatile and capable of solving many problems quickly. The team has a learning-by-doing attitude, since they together can solve many problems and create solutions that did not exist before. This reduces coordination challenges since the dependencies between functional areas changes in nature. Because there is actually one individual per functional area on a team, it is easier for individuals to relay information from the team to the rest of the functional area. This approach also reduces the loss of knowledge between functional areas and contribute to a decision-making process that is more streamlined and transparent. As a result, there is less blame and more pro-active behavior. Over time, as more and more individuals collaborate with one another, their own skill sets and knowledge bases are broadened. The best possible outcome is that the individuals take ownership of the project because they had been involved with the project from start to finish.

It is important to either hire who can work on T-shaped teams or train individuals to work on T-shaped teams. Of course, it is preferable to hire T-shaped professionals from the onset but this is difficult since many individuals receive traditional training and degrees. Although it is difficult to detect empathy from reviewing one's resume, it is easier to detect empathy when meeting the individual whether this occurs formally through the interview process or informally when casually meeting someone. Empathy can be seen when the individual talks positively about other people with whom they have collaborated. If an individual focuses and talks only on their own accomplishments, then it is a red flag. However, if an individual talks positively about team experiences or how others have helped them to accomplish their own goals, then it is a sign of empathy. Relatedly, for individuals are already at the company, one way to detect empathy is to pay attention to the individuals who are always being recruited to various teams. It is a sign that their peers appreciate their collaborative nature and that their knowledge and skill sets are sound. It is also important to pay attention to how people participate in the organization and in the wider service ecosystem. Are they contributing in various places? Are they good members of the community? Are they sharing their knowledge and giving advice? It is also a good idea to develop a 360-degree review, which can evaluate how well the individual has maintained and updated their deep knowledge base and skill set. A 360-degree review can also assess whether they have developed collaboration and communication skills, as well as other skills related to working on teams.

Scholarly and Managerial Takeaway

The purpose of this chapter is to explore the nuances of innovation as they occur at the micro level. This includes exploring what innovation looks like at the micro level, as well as describing and focusing on individuals as innovators. Traits of great innovators are also discussed. Much of the research in this area suggests that trust is an underlying condition for innovation.

References

Bryant, Scott E. 2005. The Impact of Peer Mentoring on Organizational Knowledge Creation and Sharing. *Group & Organization Management* 30 (3): 319–338. https://doi.org/10.1177/1059601103258439.

Chandler, Jennifer D., et al. 2018. How Does Innovation Emerge in a Service Ecosystem? *Journal of Service Research* 22 (1): 75–89. https://doi.org/10.1177/1094670518797479.

Fleming, Lee, et al. 2007. Collaborative Brokerage, Generative Creativity, and Creative Success. *Administrative Science Quarterly* 52 (3): 443–475. https://doi.org/10.2189/asqu.52.3.443.

Grant, Robert M. 1996. Toward a Knowledge-Based Theory of the Firm. *Strategic Management Journal* 17 (S2): 109–122. https://doi.org/10.1002/smj.4250171110.

Powell, Walter W., et al. 1996. Interorganizational Collaboration and the Locus of Innovation: Networks of Learning in Biotechnology. *Administrative Science Quarterly* 41 (1): 116. https://doi.org/10.2307/2393988.

Satell, Greg. 2018. 4 Ways to Build an Innovative Team. *Harvard Business Review*, February 13. hbr.org/2018/02/4-ways-to-build-an-innovative-team

Van De Ven, Andrew H., and Marshall Scott Poole. 1990. Methods for Studying Innovation Development in the Minnesota Innovation Research Program. *Organization Science* 1 (3): 313–335. https://doi.org/10.1287/orsc.1.3.313.

Zheng, Wei, et al. 2010. How Do Leadership and Context Matter in R&D Team Innovation? – A Multiple Case Study. *Human Resource Development International* 13 (3): 265–283. https://doi.org/10.1080/13678868.2010.483816.

CHAPTER 4

Innovation and Diffusion at the Meso Level

As discussed in Chap. 3, individuals reach out to one another when attempting to solve problems in their unique contexts. Through this process, individuals often become affiliated with one another in a social, economic, or psychological relationship. As a result, the two actors and the relationship between them can be considered a dyad. Based on this, as discussed in Chap. 3, dyads are often the focal points of a micro-level perspective of service ecosystems because they are the basis for direct reciprocity in service ecosystems.

Given this, it is important to continue developing a more detailed language and measurement of context in order to better develop the researcher's perspective on the service ecosystem. This necessitates widening the lens to include actors who are connected immediately beyond the immediate dyad. To begin building this lexicon, it is helpful to define context as a unique set of actors and the unique reciprocal links among them (Chandler and Vargo 2011). By conceptualizing context in this way, it is possible to differentiate one service ecosystem from another. More importantly, it is important to generate a lexicon for describing how various service ecosystems differ from one another.

When zooming out from the micro level to the meso level, researchers refocus their investigation from dyads in the micro level to triads in the meso level. This is akin to zooming out while looking through a microscope, from the atom level to the molecule level. It entails looking at the same object or phenomenon but from a wider view. Thus, triads are sets

J. D. Chandler, *Innovation, Social Networks, and Service Ecosystems*,
https://doi.org/10.1007/978-3-030-47797-4_4

of three actors and the relationships among them (instead of dyads, which consist of two actors and the relationship between them). To investigate triads when viewing service ecosystems at the a meso-level magnification, researchers should take two steps. First, researchers should choose a focal actor and identify the dyads in which the focal actor is a member. Then, researchers should extend their lens one step out from the dyads to view the next set of actors that are connected to each of those dyads. Each dyad may be connected to multiple third actors. By doing so, researchers identify multiple triads that may be overlapping. Each triad is thus comprised of a unique set of three actors and their relationships. Moreover, there may be multiple triads connected to a focal actor. Nonetheless, the focal actor is indirectly connected to the third actors via its dyadic membership. A set of triads constitute one specific context, while another set of actors and relationships in a different set of triads may comprise a different context. It is difficult to discuss context in measureable detail, but this is a start. Traditionally, there has been an emphasis on either the individual actor or the individual ecosystem. However, there has been little focus on the magnifications "between" individual actor and the ecosystem. These sets of triads, or contexts, help to better understand service ecosystems by highlighting the middle ground of differences among service ecosystems. Moreover, focusing on triads makes it possible to identify the relationships in a context that are most fundamental for providing individual actors with access to heterogeneous resources. Stated differently, triadic membership also provides the focal actor with indirect access to resources and service vis-à-vis the middle actor that can transfer resources between either of the other two actors in a triad. Thus, triads provide first glimpses of indirect access or transfers within service ecosystems.

The ability of actors to indirectly access or transfer resources is the basis for participation in a larger service ecosystem. Without indirect access or indirect transferability, every actor in a service ecosystem would need to interact with, form relationships with, and negotiate with every other actor in the service ecosystem. This would be very time-intensive and costly. Thus, these indirect access or transfers are important in service ecosystems because they are the most fundamental mechanism for the scaling of value creation. Because triads remove the requisite direct connection for value creation, actors do not need to be directly connected to participate in value creation. Triads are also important for innovation because they exert strong influence on the focal actor and the actor's evaluation, rejection, or acceptance of a value proposition. Relatedly, the other actors embedded in the context of a focal actor help and influence the focal actor when negotiating value propositions. In this way, the other actors embedded in the context of a focal actor, intentionally or not, help the focal actor to either adapt the value proposition or reject it. In some triads, two actors may indirectly help one another by serving the same actor; the two actors may not be aware that they are helping one another. In some triads, none of the three actors may be directly connected. These are all important because direct relationships are not necessary for actors to be directly related to create value.

Understanding triad dynamics sheds light on how actors draw upon one another as resources. This is critically dependent on the contexts in which they are embedded. Actors are influenced by other actors in their contexts, and, conversely, contexts are thus influenced by the actors to whom they are connected. Because each actor is different, each actor serves as a unique resource in the triad or context. Since actors are always changing, the nature of triads is also always changing. This continuous change highlights a fluidity that is framed, or formed, by context. Context affects the resources that can be drawn upon by actors when they respond or adapt to value propositions. Every individual actor is unique and is thus connected to a unique set of triads that comprise a specific context. This context influences the ability of a focal actor to access and leverage resources since contexts are also heterogeneous and distinctive. These ideas stem from the sociology of markets and social networks literature.

For these reasons, actors and contexts are mutually constitutive in that they define one another. In other words, actors are defined by their contexts while their contexts are defined by them (the actors). However, because each actor is embedded in a different context, resources may act as advantages in particular contexts, but act as deterrents in other contexts. Accordingly, resources become more or less helpful or beneficial as a result of the context in which the focal actor is embedded. Stated differently, resources (or deterrents) may be more beneficial (or harmful) in one context but not in another.

The Importance of Value Propositions

Value propositions are especially important at the triadic context level because actors use them to invite other actors to engage. As described previously, actors reach out to one another to solve problems. When they do reach out to one another, they often offer a value propositions that offer an economic, financial, or social benefit to those who are invited. Invited actors may respond in a way that shapes or influences the value proposition, especially within the actors' immediate contexts. Because contexts encompass dyads and triads, the actors included at this magnification are typically one step out from a focal actor's immediate neighborhood of direct dyadic connections. In other words, the third actor in a triad may be unknown to the focal actor. In this way, the triad is where connections start to become impersonal. When a focal actor is not directly connected with that third actor, the other dyadic actor often acts as the connector or bridge spanner. As a result, the value proposition that was proposed emerges from a negotiation that involves sensing, evaluating, and sharing feedback among triadic actors. This negotiation is extremely important because it shapes the value proposition and emerging innovation according to the unique nature of the context.

An overlooked aspect of innovation, the negotiation of value propositions is critical for exploring how a context can emerge as an innovation. This occurs first when value propositions begin to align actors who are embedded in the same context, especially when actors who are not directly connected respond to a value proposition. When disconnected actors in a triad or context respond to a value proposition, they gain a mutual understanding of a new idea. Importantly, because the actors are loosely connected, as they shape the new idea they consequently become aligned because they come to share similar thoughts, attitudes, or intents about the innovation. In this way, the value proposition influences the actors and the context, inasmuch as the actors and the context influence the value proposition. As this is happening, the context changes while the actors themselves shape and form the value proposition according to their own unique values, attitudes, and beliefs. In this way, value propositions and contexts are also mutually constitutive.

In short, value propositions bring actors together by communicating mutual benefits and providing a mutual organizing principle that can connect actors for the long term. Actors who offer value propositions must decide on the appropriate language and benefits when communicating with others. When they do this, value propositions come to provide a lexicon for developing, conceiving, evaluating, and shaping a new idea. They guide communications and hone how promises of reciprocity evolve in specific contexts with respect to the new idea, in response to the efforts put forth by the actors in a specific context. When actors agree to the tenets of the value proposition, the value proposition may change but it also prospers. By prospering, the value proposition unites the actors in creating value. However, this does not happen because of all value propositions. This only happens for compelling value propositions that are relevant, from the perspective of a particular actor within a specific context. Compelling value propositions successfully invite actors in a context to engage in helping a new idea come to fruition. Sometimes when value propositions emerge as innovation, the intensity of engagement varies. These changes can be summarized in phases.

In the stimulation phase, new ideas are continuously introduced. At this point, compelling value propositions are very important because there is no meaning shared among those who are evaluating the value proposition. The language and lexicon offered by value propositions help to align these ideas with actors' values and beliefs. When value propositions are compelling, they draw on language and beneficial outcomes that are appealing to actors in the context and which successfully elicit the engagement of actors in that specific context.

At the start of the replication phase, actor engagement increases and a pattern of behaviors begins to emerge in the context. Some actors begin to invest themselves in new ideas and become excited about the emergent value. A cohesive pattern of behaviors, values, and beliefs becomes associated with the new idea. Actors begin to recognize how the new idea can benefit them and help them to solve problems in their unique contexts. They become engaged in replicating the value proposition to their other relationships, and momentum is generated. As they do this, they integrate resources in various ways according to the contexts in which they are embedded. In their own individual ways, the actors work toward solving their own unique problems, but together they are actually emerging an innovation. Although each actor's problems and solutions differ from those of the others, each actor's engagement catalyzes innovation albeit in different ways. First, some actors may draw on the value proposition to solve problems that help them to move toward a specific goal. Meanwhile, other actors may draw on the value proposition to solve problems related to their pasts. And finally, other actors may draw on the value proposition to solve problems in their current contexts in order to generate more meaning. In this way, each actor draws upon the value proposition in a unique way that aligns various values, meaning, actions, intentions, and behaviors with the innovation. When these become more strongly melded together, an innovation is more likely to emerge. Sometimes actors may not respond favorably to a value proposition. Or, actors may not find it fruitful to continue engaging with a value proposition. As a result, a new idea or value proposition can be dismissed or die before it permeates through a specific context. Sometimes ideas or value propositions cause shocks that ripple through contexts. When this happens, other actors may not respond favorably to a value proposition. Then, the idea or value proposition is less likely to reach a larger audience or gain a foothold in the system before it loses its potency. In these cases, the value proposition or new idea may not emerge as innovation. Nonetheless, the potency of a value proposition or new idea may have stirred contextual changes that make it possible for the next idea or value proposition to be given more positive consideration.

In the synchronization phase, compelling value propositions are important because they begin to align the engagement of multiple actors across varying contexts. The attention and resources of these actors are necessary to catapult the value proposition forward. Based on the language, values, and behaviors attached to the value proposition from previous stages, many more actors can now learn how they too can draw on the idea to solve their own problems. Actors in other contexts begin shifting in response to the emergent new patterns associated with the value proposition. At this point, many actors are now aware of and can become engaged with the value proposition. Synchronicity emerges as a high number of actors are implicitly coordinated by their engagement with the value proposition.

However, some actors may fall out of alignment with the value proposition. Simply put, when a specific problem in an actor's context cannot be solved, that actor will look for other problems to solve. Their time, attention, and energy are now diverted to other new ideas and other value propositions. As humans, this search is constantly occurring across nature because actors need to be able to cope and solve their own problems. Sometimes others see an opportunity to engage, and because of their engagement, different logics that change the nature of the value proposition cause it to lose momentum. Something external can also disrupt the momentum of a value proposition. For these reasons, value propositions do not always emerge as innovations.

Despite this, the work of the value proposition is to catalyze dialogue and negotiation so that contexts can evolve. Without the continuous introduction, evaluation, acceptance and/or rejection of value propositions, contexts would remain stagnant. New ideas would not prosper. Conflicts, lack of resources, or conflicts in meanings would not be resolved.

The same problems would remain over many years. When value propositions are not compelling, an individual actor whose engagement is necessary for value creation may choose to disengage from its context. Or, actors whose values, behaviors, or beliefs do not align with those of others may deter or impede the pattern of engagement. Because neither value propositions or contexts can be controlled, generated, or created singularly by any one particular actor, it is important to come to a deep understanding of how the complexity and richness of the two are tied together. In order to problem-solve, actors need to engage with others. They do this by offering value propositions that help them to evolve their contexts.

The meso level is important for innovation because it is where the processes of many intersect with those of many others, and ultimately build momentum for a value proposition or a new idea. Referring back to service innovation, service is about designing and creating processes that work well. When these processes can be aligned with new ideas or value propositions, value is created based on the engagement of many. The important starting block for this is the value proposition, which, again, is an invitation to engage. Value propositions bring actors together and evolve contexts so that they are dynamic and continuously changing. Value propositions engage actors by bringing their resources together in ways that are uniquely tuned to problem-solving in their own contexts. No one knows their problems better than them. It is not possible for anyone else to solve those problems, except the actors themselves. When each actor draws on their unique context to address a problem, the actor contributes meaning to the new idea. When these meanings become attached to a value proposition, the value proposition truly becomes an organizing principle. It aligns actors and their resources with an idea, and together these all jointly evolve the multiple contexts needed for an innovation to come to life. In this way, innovation does not occur by one single actor or according to one single logic; rather, innovation emerges through a complex dynamic process that is layered by the efforts of many actors to solve problems in their own contexts.

Value propositions are like living organisms in that they are always changing and adapting. Conversely, contexts are always also changing and adapting. Value propositions are like plants in a garden, while contexts are like gardens. Separate from the garden in which it is seeded, a plant can affect the soil in the garden but is also simultaneously affect by it. As the leaves, stems, and fruits of the plant develop, so too does the soil. The value proposition and its context, like the plant and its soil, form an ecosystem with all their various elements that continuously move through time together. They continuously adapt to one another. Yet, similar to some plants and the soil in which they are grown, some value propositions thrive in some contexts and fail in others. In order to evolve and emerge, they need to gain continuous access to the resources that allow them to jointly adapt. If not, then the value proposition or the context may spin out in a way that they are no longer compatible. This is not bad, since the value proposition or context may have evolved in some way that prepares it for another round. However, the process of engagement with value propositions begins again.

Value Propositions and Plasticity

Value propositions can influence plasticity, or the service ecosystem's capacity to take and retain form. They do this by influencing how well various contexts at the meso level of magnification respond to the problem reconciliation of individual actors. When viewing this at the micro level, it can look like an individual actor acting creatively or drawing on cognitive, emotional, or physical capacity to respond to a problem. When viewing this at the macro level, it can look like a service ecosystem adapting or effecting feedback loops that change its trajectory. However, when viewing this at the meso level, it can look like an individual actor reaching out to other actors in his or her network in order to solve a problem.

When value propositions influence the service ecosystem's capacity to take and retain form, it is actually the actors within a context that are changing their abilities to move in a different direction and create a different trajectory toward a future inspired by the value proposition. This begins when individual actors may attempt to reconcile problems in their own contexts by learning about other actors' beliefs, emotions, and cognitions regarding the problems they have identified. While other actors may disagree with a potential solution or may not see an issue as a problem, the actors engaged with the value proposition may advocate for his or her viewpoint. By doing so, the actor is influencing his or her context. The actor adjusts his or her efforts accordingly, which creates a feedback loop facilitated by service ecosystem plasticity. This enhances the fluidity of the service ecosystem by helping it to take on a new form.

Meanwhile, the focal actor's attempts to solve his or her own problems are now directed toward facilitating how other actors might draw on the value proposition in ways that are meaningful in their own personal contexts. For instance, the focal actor may attempt to create awareness about the value proposition in a way that highlights its benefits to other actors. This feedback loop transpires as a form of learning in that actors realize how the value proposition can help. At the same time, this feedback loop introduces more stability to the service ecosystem by helping users agree to a joint solution. To further enhance service ecosystem fluidity, the focal actor may also attempt to disassociate the values and beliefs that do not coincide with a new idea. They attempt to create feedback loops that facilitate knowledge sharing in order to make these issues salient. These are crucial for temporarily increasing the fluidity of the service ecosystem in order to disrupt its current trajectory. The value proposition—which is essentially an idea—is an attempt to solve a problem in a highly fluid service ecosystem. The attempts to solve the problem are remembered in the service ecosystem, although an actual solution may not actually emerge. In this way, the innovation process is cyclical since it easily and continually returns to the idea phase when solutions do not emerge. As the development process of a solution persists over time, the service ecosystem eventually does take on a new or different form. It recursively begins to revolve around new values, beliefs, or behaviors, especially when actors in the context of the focal actor begin to coalesce around new norms, rules, or beliefs. When this occurs, there is social pressure to conform to these new norms, rules or beliefs. These efforts however take time. When a focal actor enlists macro-level tools to create awareness and support for a solution, the focal actor capitalizes on service ecosystem fluidity by disrupting current values, norms, beliefs, and behaviors that are perceived to be misaligned with the new idea. Although these attempts may have occurred in the past, the associated changes are deposited and transmitted throughout the service ecosystem over time. Then, when more and more users become aware of new norms and beliefs, the system as whole adapts more easily and readily to the value proposition.

In a similar vein, complementarity enhances system plasticity when actors in the immediate context of the focal actor begin to improve the capacity of the service ecosystem to take a different form by allowing for the problem to be addressed. They do this by stabilizing emergent norms, rules, and beliefs and also by engaging others in their efforts. These newly engaged actors ultimately can also lend their resources to supporting the emergent logic. In shorter feedback loops, these actors became newly aligned with the potential solution and often work in their own unique ways to evolve related institutions to the new ideas or beliefs. Through a recursive process of multiple feedback loops, other ecosystem actors learn about the idea and gradually establish mechanisms to stabilize others in their own unique contexts around a new solution. While these efforts to stabilize a service ecosystem around a solution emerge, they also facilitate shorter, faster feedback loops that can bring other contexts into closer alignment with the values, beliefs, and policies that would bring the value proposition to life. Although individual actors may still doubt or resist the new idea or solution, the idea evolves more convincingly toward the solution phase. It is especially important that actors in the context of the focal actor can relate to the new idea as helping them to also improve their own situations in some way. This mutuality helps to bond loosely, indirectly connected actors to one another. This stabilizes nascent norms, rules, and beliefs that are fundamental for the service ecosystem to retain a new form.

On a related note, when a focal actor sees that issues are not completely resolved, then that actor returns back to the idea phase to continue working on offering a more enticing solution. Having interacted with others in their contexts, these actors now go to back to the drawing board with different thoughts about the initial problem and potential solution. Another type of feedback loop, this effort coalesces assemblages of disparate thoughts, beliefs, or ideas into new efforts, which inform subsequent rounds of institutional work that are informed by actors from all over the service ecosystem. When potential solutions radiate from the focal actor, they often permeate neighboring contexts, which might also then stimulate related or similar innovation processes throughout the service ecosystem. This greatly influences the plasticity of a service ecosystem. This fundamental process of diffusion underscores the role of plasticity in the recursive, systemic nature of innovation.

Managerial Aspects of Value Propositions

From a practical perspective, it is important for managers to think comprehensively about value propositions and the role that value propositions might play in their own firms. More specifically, it is important to consider how socialization can detract from or enhance the likelihood of accepting new value propositions or ideas. To begin with, effective socialization can help actors feel comfortable and confident when they consider new ideas and different ways of doing things. When individuals are encouraged to share advice, they are more likely to take responsibility and accountability for their own behaviors related to innovation. Moreover, when they offer knowledge or information that is helpful to others in the organization, they are ultimately sharing their own values, norms, and beliefs. When these are relevant for accepting value propositions or new ideas, these behaviors can shape the evaluation and reception of a new idea or value proposition.

It is also important that these actors feel comfortable giving advice to other individuals who may not be on their current teams. This is because boundary spanning behaviors help to create an organizational culture of openness and innovation. Managers should work to cultivate these behaviors by reaching out personally to individuals who are knowledgeable and encouraging them to share their values, knowledge, and wisdom with others. Managers can also facilitate advice-giving by creating and supporting mentoring programs that explicitly assign advice-givers to the advice-giving role for more junior actors. This helps to create an organizational culture that is more integrated across different teams and social cohorts. When social connections are more prevalent in an organization, there is likely to be more knowledge and information sharing. Conversely, it is also important for managers to encourage actors to seek advice from other actors. Again, a formal mentoring program can facilitate this behavior but it is also important to ensure an environment and organizational culture that promotes psychological safety.

Many organizations employ socialization tactics that occur outside the traditional work day. These are important efforts since they improve social bonding and create an atmosphere of safety. While it is acceptable for managers to assume that socialization should occur after work, at retreats, or on weekends, it is equally important that socialization also occur within the traditional work day. Managers can facilitate this when individuals are given ample time, opportunity, and space to interact both casually, or informally, and formally or with respect to their explicit work roles. Doing so can hone the valued culture of advice-giving that leads to innovation. Within the work day, in addition to formal meetings, it can be fruitful to provide a few minutes or opportunities for individual-level social interactions over morning or afternoon coffee. These budding relationships can be the seeds of innovation.

It may be beneficial to deter the transfer of explicit knowledge as part of the socialization process. Explicit knowledge is not affiliated with value propositions; rather, explicit knowledge centers on enforcing rules, norms, and values. When explicit knowledge is discussed among actors, there is less discussion of new ideas. Instead of encouraging discussion of explicit knowledge, managers can expedite explicit knowledge transfer by posting this knowledge for display on internal websites. Social chatting applications can decrease the amount of time spent on explicit knowledge transfer so that individuals are not inundated with requests for explicit knowledge. Explicit knowledge, which is typically housed in "Frequently Asked Questions (FAQ)," can also be cataloged through the use of data warehouses and information systems. This may help to dislodge information bottlenecks and open up the information process capabilities of individuals who become prominent in explicit knowledge networks.

Managers should also work to present value propositions to teams of teams because innovation is positively influenced when individuals across project teams interact with one another regardless of their team affiliations, rather than only with their respective project teams. Socialization plays a very important role in making this happen and has significant consequences for innovation within project-based organizations.

Socialization has been shown to be an important resource for those seeking a competitive advantage through innovation. Although socialization has been shown to lead to many positive organizational outcomes, it has not previously been linked to the evaluation and acceptance of value propositions. This is because individual actors who are constantly assembled and reassembled onto different project teams interact with a wide variety of actors as they evaluate value propositions. Managers need to ensure that the knowledge, ideas, and information generated in association with a value proposition be comprehensively dispersed throughout the organization in order to maximize innovation. Socialization tactics facilitate individuals seeking advice and strengthen friendship across an organization, which enhances psychological safety, trust, and reciprocity—all of which have been shown in extant research to positively influence the acceptance of new ideas and, ultimately, innovation. Innovation can be positively influenced by cultivating specific behaviors vis-à-vis socialization across different project teams, not only within a project team. This emphasizes the core tenets of innovation as an organization's ability to generate a recombination of knowledge in new ways. This can be enhanced by advice-giving and friendship among individuals in an organization, regardless of their project team affiliation. These results should encourage managers to examine more deeply the norms and beliefs that characterize project-based organizations in order to identify the specific behaviors that make project-based organizations more innovative overall. Furthermore, these results should also encourage managers to engage socialization tactics that shape the norms, rules, and beliefs of an organization to promote more advice-giving across project teams. In project-based organizations, socialization is an important driver of innovation that requires further investigation.

Plasticity, or a service ecosystem's capacity to take and retain form, influences how well a context can adapt to change and consequently transmit the effects of innovation to the wider service ecosystem. By viewing value propositions through an institutional lens, it can be seen that plasticity influences how well a focal actor's efforts to reconcile institutions are received within its own unique context. It is not necessary for all actors in a context to agree with one another; for example, some actors may feel concerned about a potential solution or new idea, while others may feel optimistic or energized by it. However, it is the dialogue between those two actors that can help to refine an idea. As the focal actor gains momentum, the actor's attempts to solve his or her own problems are now focused on creating awareness about the proposed solution and persuading others that this solution can also help them to address their own personal needs and purposes. This feedback loop catalyzes a form of learning in that actors arrive at a better understanding of their own situations, which in turn introduces more stability to the service ecosystem. They come to a joint acknowledgment that the solution can be successful. Service ecosystem fluidity is enhanced when the focal actor works to dislodge the extant context from the moral foundations—including values, beliefs, and attitudes—that are associated with current paradigms and institutions. Actors in the context jointly attempt, though in their own unique ways, to create feedback loops that facilitate knowledge sharing and enhanced learning about the solution. This facilitates continuous feedback loops that disseminate, as well as converge, disparate but related ideas throughout the service ecosystem. The context is important at this point because there needs to be a wider adaptation to the solution in order for it to continue evolving. This temporary increase in the fluidity of the service ecosystem promotes disruption of the prevailing institutional order.

A solution—that appears initially as an idea—often emerges from a focal actor's catalyzed attempts to solve his or her own problems in a highly fluid service ecosystem. These attempts to solve problems from the past affect the context and are thus deposited there, although the actual development of a solution may have stalled or been deterred from further dissemination throughout the service ecosystem. Sometimes, a solution is not yet ready for the context to which it was introduced, or, vice versa, and sometimes a context is not yet ready for the solution. In these cases, the solution is ultimately returned to the figurative “drawing board” and the innovation process begins again. However, as the development of a solution persists over time, there is a series of nonlinear feedback loops in the context that help the service ecosystem to take different forms. That is, as a context morphs and adapts to a solution, the service ecosystem—from a macro-level perspective—appears to take different forms. Recursively, the context and service ecosystem begin to spiral and center toward the values, norms, and beliefs associated with the solution. This may occur as actors in a context continuously exert social persuasion efforts to help the new idea or solution gain acceptance. By starting to mobilize macro-level support for a solution in this way, the focal actor builds on the fluidity of the service ecosystem. The context may endure disruption in values, norms, beliefs, and behaviors that are perceived to be misaligned with the solution. Nonetheless, the effects accumulate in the meta-space and then are transmitted throughout the service ecosystem. Then, more and more actors become aware of or familiar with new norms and beliefs.

In a similar vein, other actors in the context can increase the capacity of a service ecosystem to continue in a new form by giving stability to emergent norms, values or beliefs. This stabilization might occur when other actors show support for a new idea or solution. This creates a shorter feedback loop that aligns other actors in the same context with the proposed solution. As this occurs outward in all directions, the proposed solution gains traction with similar feedback loops that move the holistic service ecosystem closer toward the values, norms beliefs, and policies associated with the solution. A recursive process, this diffusion permeates to other service ecosystem actors and gradually establishes fundamental mechanisms that change the service ecosystem nature and help to stabilize the service ecosystem around the new idea. During this time, the efforts of the focal actor were complemented by the attempts of others in the same context to solve his or her own problems. These efforts were necessary to stabilize competing but still nascent norms, rules, and beliefs and to improve the ecosystem’s capacity to retain a new form.

Soon, the larger set of actors that have now adopted the new idea may realize that their issues were not completely reconciled and return back to the idea phase to continue moving toward an improved solution. They renew institutionalized feedback loops and adapt subsequent rounds of institutional work. As a result, each return to the drawing board meant that further institutional work would generate entirely different ideas that stemmed from learning from actors that are located in other contexts all over the service ecosystem.

Multisided Platforms as a Context

Since data, social media, and technology are everywhere in the twenty-first-century economy, multisided platforms have become an important context to consider. In service ecosystems and the new economy, multisided platforms are technologies, products, or services that enable direct interactions between two or more groups that would not have otherwise been able to interact (Hagiu and Wright 2015). These platforms facilitate indirect access and transfer of resources by connecting two or more groups together. eBay is a good example of a multisided platforms because it joins together buyers and sellers around the world. Buyers and sellers are directly connected to eBay, and eBay is the bridge or broker between the buyers and the sellers. eBay facilitates indirect access and transfer of resources; without eBay, interactions among buyers and sellers obviously would not occur at all. Other multisided platforms include a shopping mall or Farmer's Market, Snapchat, or Netflix.

Multisided platforms essentially reduce the search costs of finding adequate direct interactions for both buyers and sellers. Paypal, for example, generates revenue by centering its business model on helping buyer and sellers make indirect connections to each other, with Paypal as the mid-point. Paypal, like other multisided platforms, completes the triad that includes the buyer, seller, and eBay. Without Paypal, the triad would not exist. If one were to consider the context surrounding PayPal, it would include those in the immediate neighborhood of Paypal. Thus, the success of PayPal rests on its buyers and sellers as these are the actors in its own context.

This is especially clear in the situation of Netflix. As a multisided platform, Netflix viewers can find movies, documentaries, and television shows to watch. Essentially, Netflix brings this content into the context of home viewership. In this way, multisided platforms like Netflix reduce transaction costs by decreasing the need for "search." In other words, Netflix brings context (i.e., viewers) to content, and vice versa content to the home context. Most important, Netflix generates revenue by charging service fees rather than by acting as a third-party retailer that sells products and facilitates the exchange of ownership. In the same way, Facebook creates a context when it joins content generators with content viewers.

Although they are separated by physical space, Facebook brings these into the same context.

Multisided platforms play an important role in the Internet economy because they reduce search costs and transaction costs. They do this by making it easier and cheaper to find the third actor to complete a triad. In triads that are made complete by a multisided platform, there are network externalities which yield benefit for those in the triad based on the size of the groups that are indirectly connected. For example, Netflix and Facebook viewers typically benefit when there is more content to view. Conversely, Netflix and Facebook content generators typically benefit when there are more viewers to see their content. The multisided platform creates a content that makes these network externalities possible. This results in a cycle that is perpetuated when an increasing number of actors (both content providers and viewers) join the service ecosystem. However, negative network externalities may also emerge when the benefits of the service ecosystem decrease due to the size of either groups becoming too large.

Essentially, multisided platforms can be viewed as value propositions since they act as invitations to engage in a particular context or service ecosystem. The value proposition, however, becomes difficult to evaluate because the benefit is not typically based on size; rather it is based on the heterogeneity within groups. In other words, within each group, there needs to be a sufficient variety of viewers and content generators, or buyers and sellers. Size alone is not sufficient to guarantee whether the value proposition will succeed. If there is not enough content, then value will not exist for viewers. Conversely, if there are not enough viewers, then value will not exist for content generators. With respect to size, generally speaking in systems research, this generally refers to threshold or capacity issue because it is usually assumed that the size effect drives the ability of information systems to function. However, for multisided platforms, heterogeneity within any of the groups can influence network externalities.

Because of this, generally speaking, it is challenging to price membership, subscription, or participation in a multisided platform. Since multisided platforms do not facilitate ownership or exchange of goods, they can be more fruitfully managed using the principles of incomplete products. Incomplete products are based on the "freemium" model in which an intellectual property (usually content such as video game or music license) is given to customers for free, albeit in a complete state. In other words, the full value of the intellectual property can only be fully realized if and/

or when the customer purchases content add-ons through often multiple rounds of microtransactions. This same approach is used in smartphone applications, which are often free in a basic format, but are available with upgrades and special features for a paid purchase or subscription. This approach has been successful in stimulating excitement, interest, and sampling of new products and services. For example, massive multiplayer online games (MMOG) have garnered significant success by utilizing the freemium approach to video games on mobile devices. In the past, most video games were limited to video game consoles and cartridges that were high in cost. Increasingly, MMOGs started to require fast Internet broadband services and strong processing power. MMOGs such as Fortnite are now accessible on smartphones using cellular connections as players move freely throughout their days in a nonstop play fashion. Building on the "freemium" approach, Fortnite was easily accessible and free for players to use. But then players would become angry when they were unable to advance through the game because they were not able to make additional purchases that would help them to advance through the game. So, although the number of players was increasing, the "freemium" level of content that was available at no charge was limited. Similarly, because the game required other players to already play the game (hence the massive multiplayer online game aspect), game developers used artificially intelligent "bots" to "play" the game against or with first movers. Gamers became cynical when they learned that they mostly played against bots rather than other gamers in the service ecosystem. In the end, the group was angered and ultimately became discouraged from engaging with the platform at all.

On a similar note, servitization refers to a new emphasis on long-term relationship between a company and a firm based on ongoing service or upgrades to the product. This is analogous to an appliance or automobile warranty that, when purchased, includes service for a specific time and under a specified set of conditions. Warranties are carefully created to accompany the point of sale for large ticket items, and, traditionally, have been regarded as an extra, bonus, or upsell resulting from a savvy interpersonal sales pitch. However, servitization views this entire process as an inclusive package and extends the scope of "transaction" to include all of the possible services that may occur after the purchase of the original product. Understanding the nuances of freemium and servitization models helps to shed light on multisided platforms because the true value of engaging with multisided platforms is based on an ongoing engagement over time; however, pricing, service delivery, and distribution strategies for multisided platforms are still new to the twenty-first-century economy.

Looking toward the future of multisided platforms, it seems that governance will continue to be an importance issue. The success of a platform is in its ability to scale. Because of this, hundreds, thousands, and millions of actors can be involved in a particular multisided platform. For most platforms, the more actors participating makes for an even more successful platform. However, in order for all of those actors to continue generating value for themselves and others on the platform, they need to behave in a particular way. But there is currently no way to ethically and realistically expect these actors to behave in that way all of the time. In multisided platforms, governance can range from zero overarching control to 100% complete and total control. In a multisided platform that has no governance rules imparted by a central authority, the service ecosystem becomes internally determined according to the principles of synergetics. There is implicit coordination by actors in the service ecosystem and the smaller parts emerge as order parameters through consensualization as mentioned previously in this book.

Multisided Platforms as Contexts within Service Ecosystems

The principles of synergetics can help to explain how multisided platforms provide a specific context within service ecosystems. Each multisided platform can be thought of as a specific context with its specific subgroups that are joined together by unique expectations, norms, rules, and behaviors. Within each platform, actors hang together more tightly and are more densely connected. But across platforms, actors may be loosely connected and more disparate. Nonetheless, these platforms together comprise a service ecosystem. Together, the many different multisided platforms give a unique character to the entire comprehensive service ecosystem yet each multisided platform is unique in its own way. Each platform contributes to the service ecosystem in the same way that each service ecosystem contributes to each platform. Because of this, it is possible to better understand the service ecosystem by understanding each of the platforms. The dynamics of the entire service ecosystem is largely influenced by the dynamics of each platform. This is important because it is not sufficient to only recognize the role of time and the incessant interactivity among actors in a service ecosystem. Rather, it is fundamental to creatively think about the complexity and nonlinearity that emerges when actors of all types affect one another in unexpected ways.

Multisided platforms, like Amazon, Xbox, and Facebook, join actors together within contexts. Within each of these contexts, value propositions initially join actors together in their micro-environments but then ultimately connect them to others who also accept the value proposition. When this occurs, those actors come to share similar values. These platforms contribute to the service ecosystem itself because of these values, norms, beliefs, and ideologies. It is important to note these values, norms, beliefs, and ideologies—despite physical space and geodesic distance—impart a logic into the service ecosystem. When united by shared values, norms, beliefs, and ideologies, disparate (seemingly disconnected) actors garner a propensity to act in accordance with those values, norms, beliefs, and ideologies since they are supported in their "contexts." When left ungoverned, the values, norms, beliefs, and ideologies emerge in such a way that they become internally determined through a series of nonlinear feedback loops. This strengthens the values, norms, beliefs, and ideologies. This itself is not problematic; however, it may become problematic for the system as a whole if each of the various contexts evolves according to a different logic. When a context becomes too different or isolated from other contexts in the same service ecosystem, the service ecosystem at a macro level can be thrown into disarray suddenly or it may degenerate to decay. This is the kind of social change that brews quietly under the radar. This is because the service ecosystem as a whole continues to thrive and move forward through time, although the various order parameters that eventually emerge as governance mechanisms often do so through silent consensualization and quiet acquiescence from the various actors within each context. Without an explicit control mechanism imparting some agreed-upon logic, most systems tend to decay. This is only natural. Ultimately, each service ecosystem—even the global worldwide service ecosystems—comes to a day of reckoning when the institutional dissonance among contexts becomes so prevalent that there must be some form of overt negotiation across the disparate contexts in order for the service ecosystem to survive.

The various platforms exert influences on the parameters of the service ecosystem, including how the service ecosystem propagates itself and evolves over time. By understanding the order parameters (internally determined) or governance mechanisms (externally determined) of each platform or context, it can become clear how each of these multisided platforms might influence the service ecosystem. Conversely, it can also become clear how the service ecosystem might influence each multisided platform. This is because each context essentially acts like an unfinished or incomplete product until a critical mass in the service ecosystem completes it. A multisided platform simply cannot function without sufficient size and heterogeneity. Because of this, each platform or context needs to pull in actors from the service ecosystem as a whole, or, in another way of thinking about it, from other platforms or contexts. In this way, each multisided platform contributes to servitization by creating new benchmarks and best practices.

The value of contexts is that they connect service ecosystems together. Within contexts, the tight connections are important to cultivating the shared values, norms, beliefs, and ideologies that make a service ecosystem resilient. Across contexts, the loose distant connections are important for dispersing different values, norms, beliefs, and ideologies that make a service ecosystem open enough for innovation. The study of contexts, platforms, and service ecosystems is essentially the study of value, so it is important to consider how and why actors in each of these come together for mutual benefit. For this reason, it is important to note the variety of pivots or modes that are associated with multisided platforms. For instance, Amazon uses pricing and the pursuit of profit as a governance mechanism for its buyers and sellers. By setting percentages and taking sellers' costs while charging buyers for subscriptions, Amazon implicitly governs actors in their behaviors. More specifically, a seller would not want to lose margins or buyers, while a seller would not want to overpay for an item or be limited to a smaller set of choices. In this way, a pricing mechanism can change the entire logic of the service ecosystem.

Although the context that emerges around a multisided platform often serves as the consensualization for an order parameter to emerge in the service ecosystem, value is an order parameter that always stimulates evolution in the service ecosystem. In other words, it may take time for an order parameter to emerge. However, value is instantaneous in that it exists of the service ecosystem as a systemic property. Value rises from the interactions and relationships among actors in a service ecosystem. Once there is an interaction, there is value, or some benefit to the actors involved in the interaction. So when these many interactions in a service ecosystem change over time, so too does value. As a result, it is impossible to always repeat the same action over and over again, and continue to expect that action to generate the same effect or benefit. All interactions in a service ecosystem are always changing. In other words, change is the only constant and temporality is the only true connection that endures. For example, a friendship may change over time, and though the two actors who are friends may, one day, not be friends anymore, they will always have shared trajectory through time at some point. Take for instance another types of relational connection that is a group membership—a connection to many others that is based on kinship. Regardless of how the actual connection changes, the actors remain connected through time and also with one another.

For this reason, it is important to also consider the dispositions of an actor's psychological states; in other words, it is important to consider one's orientations toward the past, present, and future. These dispositions influence how an actor can draw upon his or her context. When an actor is not able to draw upon his or her context in a way that orients them appropriately toward the past, present, or future, they become disengaged from the service ecosystem. When an actor is able to draw upon his or her context in a way that propels them toward a desired past, present, or future, they engage even more in the service ecosystem.

Context is important because it is comprised of a focal actors' connections (temporal and relational) and dispositions (orientation toward the past, present, and future). Based on an actor's context, the actor typically decides whether and how to engage in the wider service ecosystem. When connects and dispositions are aligned and synchronized, an actor can be more fully engaged in his or her or its context. This is because value is the primary order parameter and the actor knows how to draw upon his or context in order to gain some benefit. However, connections and dispositions continually fall out of alignment, and it is naturally difficult to maintain synchronicity. Alignment of connections and dispositions naturally shifts over time, especially in response to the actor, the service ecosystem, and value.

Service ecosystems can be reframed by thinking about synergetics. Its principles of *critical distance* and *stability* explain system behaviors when the system is at *equilibrium*. At equilibrium, connections and dispositions are aligned. At equilibrium, it is simple and easy to maintain extant logics of value co-creation. This is because the propensity of the service ecosystem simply needs to keep doing what it has been doing, and operate according to the existing logics or order parameters. Since this propensity tends to be resistant to change, the service ecosystem as a whole resists and wards off anomalous perturbations or possible changes.

Despite this, in transition phases that occur in the early stages of service ecosystems, the principles of *amplification* and *internal determination* describe fluctuations and their influence on service ecosystems. First, random changes appear and then begin to change how specific dynamics occur. Then, unique order parameters of a service ecosystem begin to emerge. In this way, service ecosystems differentiate from other service ecosystems because of the way that they respond to change; that is, their plasticity determines how much they change, especially in response to external forces. If there is a strong but secluded multisided platform at the center of the service ecosystem, it typically propels these dynamics. Each service ecosystem is unique and complex. Every behavior matters. Differences in these behaviors show how a jolt in the multisided platform, or a change in logic of the functionality of the multisided platform, can reverberate throughout the entire service ecosystem.

It is important to account for the myriad of ways that service ecosystems react back on themselves through many repetitive nonlinear feedback loops. These loops are the pivots that often cause logics to shift and orders to unravel in service ecosystems. As the loops permeate the ecosystem, they exert small forces in some places and large multiplier effects in other places. These stimulate shifts in service ecosystems that move them from one state to another, and back again. Essentially, this is how service ecosystems move from a point of equilibrium to the next equilibrium. Even though the characteristics of the service ecosystem may change during that time, it is still possible for the service ecosystem to become balanced and stable under new circumstances. As a result, varying components, subsequent relationships and other actors throughout the service ecosystem react or change in response.

Last, but not least, it is important to realize when *new systemic orders* emerge and catalyze *symmetry breaking*. When this occurs, *limited predictability* and *historical dependence* can be seen in the service ecosystem. When new patterns become established, new orders come to light, and varying components of the service ecosystem become consensualized in the same logic as the new pattern. Due to symmetry breaking, emergences become order parameters, which in turn shape the various components and properties of the system. These emergences are unpredictable; it is simply not possible to make a comprehensive prediction of how new systemic orders will emerge. Despite this, the principle of historical dependence asserts that past behaviors in a service ecosystem are the best foreshadows of the future trajectory of the service ecosystem.

It should be noted that most systems tend toward decay and chaos. Despite this, some service ecosystems may move toward equilibrium by enslaving its smaller components. As this occurs in service ecosystems, the distinguishing characteristics among customers, employees, and machines disappear and these various types of actors begin to look more similar. In other words, all actors can then be viewed as actors in the system. This can be helpful in the twenty-first century where robots are taking over human roles and humans are changing how they interface in service ecosystems. Most managers still are human, adapting and responding to changes in their environments or contexts. It is difficult to ascertain how many of these managers can think at a systems perspective and tolerate the shifts that naturally occur in service ecosystems. It is important to develop this seamless perspective so that managers can better navigate system phase transitions with less disruptions and stress. To this end, the Cynefin framework proposes a similar decision-making heuristic (Snowden 2002). The heuristic asserts and categorizes situational scenarios to simplify managerial decision-making according to simple, complicated, complex, chaotic, and disorder situations. Each of these scenarios varies from situations wherein cause and effect are clear, to situations in which cause and effect are ambiguous. From systems theory and complexity, the framework stems from acknowledging the various perspectives of managers and their potential behavioral response and tolerance to various levels of chaos and order. It is important to be able to develop this type of sense-making as service ecosystems become more commonplace in the twenty-first-century economy.

Data as a Context that Brings Actors Together

By taking a systems perspective on innovation, it becomes more salient how different actors come together overall. However, in modern society, one of the most important systems that brings actors together is that of data and technological systems. Service science is the study of "value-co-creation configurations of people, technology, value propositions" (Maglio and Spohrer 2008, p. 18). When it comes to artificial intelligence, machine learning, analytics, big data, and privacy, many "value co-creation configurations" emerge around data. Humans, technological devices, software, and nonhuman actors come together because of data; they are able to participate in innovation because they are linked by data. Data is a context; it is a specific set of actors and links that bring devices, software, and screens together for innovation without explicit human intervention. This chapter explores how data and multisided platforms or technologies enable direct interactions among multiple otherwise disconnected groups in a context for innovation (Hagiu 2014; Hagiu and Wright 2015).

The "DIKW pyramid" is used to conceptualize data (D) as the foundation of information (I), knowledge (K), and wisdom (W). At the bottom of the DIKW pyramid, data are "symbols that represent the properties of objects and events". Data, in this sense, are symbols that represent occurrences in the human world. As data have become digital, they have become uniform across devices, software, hardware, organizations, and societies. As a result, digital data have been able to connect together disparate groups, organizations, and societies. In short, digital data are the common threads that allow and facilitate communication across the world. These digital symbols, which are actually patterns of 0s and 1s, can be compiled as "information," which is then processed to improve the usefulness and value of the symbols. The data can sometimes take the form of larger data assemblages such as files and photos. Digital objects such as files and photos can be mixed with different material and nonmaterial components; they can become embedded in a complex digital ecosystem that enables them to be manipulated. In this way, data enriches how actors connect with one another. Through technologies such as desktop computers, sensors, personal computing devices, and smartphones, data are persistently and ubiquitously being uploaded to shared servers in the cloud. Because of the uniformity of data, the digital objects and assemblages of data are easily accessible to various types of actors, including other humans, organizations, governments, and institutions. Specifically, personal data emerge when organizations design and orchestrate the collection of data about human contexts and events. Although personal data are processed initially as information, then eventually inform how organizations perceive and respond to the world. Because of this, data join actors together in new ways.

Managerial Takeaways

To facilitate this process, managers should consider how to increase trust in their organizations. These are important managerial hints about socialization tactics that can lead to innovation. To begin with, it is important to build advice-giving behaviors in order to facilitate innovation. This implies that individuals should feel confident in their ability to offer advice and that they should offer knowledge or information that is helpful to others in the organization. Moreover, it is important that these individuals feel comfortable doing so with individuals who may not be on their current teams. In order to cultivate these behaviors, managers should reach out personally to individuals who are knowledgeable and encourage them to share their wisdom with others. It can also help to facilitate advice-giving by creating mentoring programs that explicitly assign advice-givers to the advice-giving role. Conversely, it is also important to encourage individuals to seek advice from others. Again, a formal mentoring program can facilitate this behavior but it is also important to ensure an environment that promotes psychological safety. Many organizations employ socialization tactics that occur outside the traditional work day, and assume that socialization should occur after work, at retreats, or on weekends. However, it is equally important that within the traditional work day, individuals are given ample time, opportunity, and space to interact both casually, or informally, and formally, or with respect to their explicit work roles. Doing so can hone the valued culture of advice-giving that leads to innovation. Within the work day, in addition to formal meetings, it can be fruitful to provide a few minutes or opportunities for individual-level social interactions over morning or afternoon coffee. These budding relationships can be the seeds of innovation.

It may also be beneficial to expedite the transfer of explicit knowledge by translating this knowledge from database format to display on internal websites. Social chatting applications can decrease the amount of time spent on explicit knowledge transfer so that individuals are not inundated with requests for explicit knowledge. Explicit knowledge, which is typically housed in "Frequently Asked Questions (FAQ)," can also be cataloged through the use of data warehouses and information systems. This may help to dislodge information bottlenecks and open up the information process capabilities of individuals who become prominent in explicit knowledge networks.

Most important, innovation is positively influenced when individuals across project teams interact with one another regardless of their team affiliations, rather than only with their respective project teams. Socialization plays a very important role in making this happen and has significant consequences for innovation within project-based organizations. Socialization has been shown to be an important resource for project-based organizations seeking a competitive advantage through innovation. Although socialization has been shown to lead to many positive organizational outcomes, it has not previously been linked to innovation in project-based organizations. Socialization is an especially important determinant of innovation in project-based organizations because individuals are constantly assembled and reassembled onto different project teams. Although the work of project teams takes place within the confines of a project team, it is important for the knowledge, ideas, and information generated from the project to be comprehensively dispersed throughout the organization in order to maximize innovation. Despite this, however, many top-level executives continue to prioritize and concern themselves with innovation on each of their organization's teams. Scholars and managers alike need to understand that innovation overall is enhanced when socialization tactics encourage interactions that transcend across project team boundaries. It is important to address the theoretical link between socialization and innovation by outlining which outcomes of socialization are most important for innovation. Innovation in project-based organizations is positively influenced by socialization tactics that enable individuals to seek advice. Additionally, this effect is strengthened by the presence of friendship, which typically coincides with psychological safety, trust, and reciprocity—all of which have been shown in extant research to positively influence innovation. Innovation can be positively influenced by cultivating specific behaviors vis-à-vis socialization across different project teams, not only within a project team. This emphasizes the core tenets of innovation as an organization's ability to generate a recombination of knowledge in new ways. This can be enhanced by advice-giving and friendship among individuals in an organization, regardless of their project team affiliation. Scholars should examine more deeply the norms and beliefs that characterize project-based organizations in order to identify the specific behaviors that make project-based organizations more innovative overall. Furthermore, managers should engage in socialization tactics that shape the norms, rules, and beliefs of an organization to promote more advice-giving across project teams. In project-based organizations, socialization is an important driver of innovation that requires further investigation.

Managers need to think more clearly about the influence of data on their everyday duties. Data can influence innovation by influencing how manufacturing is planned and executed through artificial intelligence. In the past, many organizations relied on paper and pencil tracking, travel, and hunches about how to optimize the state and inventory of supply chains. This contributed to high costs and wasted energy, as well as an inefficient use of materials and time. However, because of data, organizations can design and build products that seamlessly monitor and communicate with one another via information systems that are integrated across organizations. This integration will facilitate rapid adoption of cloud-based technologies that collect, process, and analyze data in real time to intelligently transform how commodities traverse through manufacturing lines into and throughout supply chains. A type of service ecosystem, these constellations are expected to build on data and the use of algorithms to help manufacturers reach higher levels of productivity and quality. As a result, overall waste can be reduced while end users enjoy products that are high quality and manufactured faster at a rate that is less damaging to the environment.

With respect to sustainability, data will also allow for closer monitoring of various types of carbon footprints. Many types of actors, including individuals, organizations, and governments, can come together based on data that help them to evaluate the quickest and most cost-effective methods for achieving net zero—or, the elimination of their carbon footprints. Data creates a context that allows for seamless integration and tracking across organizational boundaries to allow for real-time monitoring and adjustment that contributes to reduced carbon emissions. This context has already begun to form a foundation for a carbon management industry aimed at eliminating carbon dioxide in the environment, offsetting energy use throughout the world and transforming how energy is used. Data brings this context together and spurs new technologies that can reduce and remove emissions. Data will also allow increased public attention and scrutiny of government policy related to carbon footprints.

Data has also tied disparate actors together into new contexts since 5G networks are increasingly allowing data to travel quickly for instantaneous delivery. In a short amount of time, there has been a significant increase in delivery services such as Uber, Amazon, and Instacart. With lightning fast Internet connectivity, autonomous bots quickly aid in the safe delivery of various goods and services within hours or even minutes. Although location-based Internet service providers limit data connectivity over large spaces, 5G networks provide for more resilient networks that provide robust dynamics contexts that are made possible because of data connectivity. For example, virtual meetings enabled by Skype or Zoom facilitate service provision in higher capacities, including education, telehealth, and business meetings. This shifts focus away from desktop and land-based connectivity toward mobile and cloud-based connectivity. As a result, many organizations can focus on distributed service provision and remote working.

It goes without saying that data has enabled a new role, and context, for robotics in many industries. Because of a new robotics application called "microfulfillment," grocery retailers can be more productive and achieve more positive returns. Microfulfillment centers can be housed in cost-effective real estate at the store level. Then robotics used downstream at a "hyper local" level allows for value to be equally captured by retailers and consumers online. Microfulfillment robotics systems can generate approximately 4000 orders a week and be housed in the back of an actual grocery store, which can ultimately help grocery retailers to grow their margins.

Perhaps the most exciting context that has emerged as a result of data uniformity is quantum computing. With quantum computing, data are expected to catalyze an entire generation of commercial devices that can maybe solve some of our most pressing and meaningful real-world issues. For example, data could possibly enable powerful devices to simulate and replicate complex chemical reactions that prompt the development of vaccines and therapeutics to address sickness, disease, and death around the world. Hopefully, these new contexts will evolve new modes of pharmaceutical development. Similar calculations based in chemistry can aid the development of novel materials that could diminish carbon emissions in transportation and across the automotive industry. Currently, the only option to fight climate change is to create alternative energy sources; however, with quantum chemistry it is possible to change the mixture or combination of chemicals and natural resources to slow climate change. Similarly, the current state of development in the pharmaceutical industry relies on experiments that use raw materials in trial and error iterative processes that are costly and time consuming. Quantum computing can shorten discovery, as well as reduce research costs.

In another context, prevention is increasingly becoming the focus of national healthcare systems in Western countries. Empowered by data, healthcare providers and end users or patients can now work together in real time to prevent disease. This creates a new context that previously did not exist. Advances in artificial intelligence and new supply chain delivery mechanisms require biological data that engineering biology can deliver through simple, low-cost tests that help individuals to identify their ailments without physically visiting a doctor's office. This will lower the burden on hospitals since only the most severe cases will need care. This will decrease, as a result, morbidity, mortality, and costs of healthcare. Because fewer infected people would leave their homes, epidemiology would change. With inexpensive diagnostic testing, individuals can be empowered to take charge of their own health without physical visits to a doctor's office or emergence room. As a result, the quality of care will improve for those who actually do need to visit a doctor's office or hospital. Based on the benefits of plant-rich, nutrient-dense diets, more doctors, nurses, support staff, and healthcare systems are using data to help end users adopt preventative health approaches using artificial intelligence and data-based interactions. With sensors, smart devices, and smartphones, it is possible for healthcare providers to see the data representing the habits and behaviors that consumers need to engage in to maintaining optimal health. This exponentially grows the collective knowledge around the effects of dietary phytonutrients on specific health and functional outcomes. End users can become more aware in real time the importance of their nutritional decisions, and how these can influence underlying health issues. Data enables end users to be proactive in seeking healthier foods that support their natural immune responses. With the availability of data, the global food industry can respond in a timely manner to offer a wide range of nutritional options. Analogously, healthcare can focus on industry and respond by promoting earth's plant intelligence for more resilient lives and to incentivize people to take care of themselves in an effort to reduce unsustainable costs.

In today's society, organizations are engaged in multiple data collection and storage efforts. In real time, various processes across disparate organizations are orchestrated. Data are continuously drawn upon for organizational decision-making.

References

Chandler, J.D., and R.F. Lusch. 2015. Service Ecosystems: A Broadened Framework and Research Agenda on Value Propositions, Engagement, and Service Experience. *Journal of Service Research 18* (1): 6–22.

Chandler, J.D., and S.L. Vargo. 2011. Contextualization and Value-In-Context: How Context Frames Exchange. *Marketing Theory 11* (1): 35–49.

Hagiu, A. 2014. Strategic Decisions for Multisided Platforms. *MIT Sloan Management Review 55* (2): 71.

Hagiu, A., and J. Wright. 2015. Multi-sided Platforms. *International Journal of Industrial Organization 43*: 162–174.

Maglio, P.P., and J. Spohrer. 2008. Fundamentals of Service Science. *Journal of the Academy of Marketing Science 36* (1): 18–20.

Snowden, D. 2002. Complex Acts of Knowing: Paradox and Descriptive Self-Awareness. *Journal of Knowledge Management 6* (2): 100–111.

CHAPTER 5

Macro: Innovation as Renovated Connections

Due to the upsurge of advanced technology, standard corporate service systems are progressively losing their humanity. In many of these cases, software, robots, and artificial intelligence are beginning to replace the roles that once belonged solely to humans. Consequently, humans have become engaged with technology and technological actors in unprecedented ways, especially when considering that on any given day humans may interact more with technological actors than with other humans. Researchers who focus on practices, engagement, and service systems can help organizations and managers think more holistically about how to better manage these situations for favorable outcomes. To create this framework, this chapter begins with literature on practices and engagement, and then links these to the literature on service ecosystems as activities that are renovated by a new idea or value proposition predominantly exhibited by humans. Owing to the fact that many marketplace situations now include both humans and technological actors interacting for broad periods of activity, it is fundamental to our understanding to develop a framework for investigating how humans and technological actors fuse together over time. All of these are then connected to the study of service systems.

This is important because exchange occurs simultaneously all over the place, everywhere, all at the same time. Society is essentially based on trade, which is the foundation for humans interacting with one another. This is not to say that society is based on capitalism since capitalism differs

J. D. Chandler, *Innovation, Social Networks, and Service Ecosystems*,
https://doi.org/10.1007/978-3-030-47797-4_5

from trade. The argument here is that humans come to flourish among and with each other because of trade and exchange. Thanks to trade humans are not completely isolated from one another; humans rarely function autonomously in isolation from other humans. In some way or form, humans are influenced by one another because we need to help one another address issues in our unique environments. In order to help one another, we trade. Over time, social systems (e.g., communication, social norms, and language) have arisen as the scaffolding that give rise to trade. Trade is thus a basic pillar for society.

Society has, however, become so complex and diverse that the fundamental essence of trade has become obscured from plain view because humans no longer trade directly, in person, with one another. Trade has become impersonal, indirect, and facilitated by service ecosystems. As we have worked to address problems or issues in our unique contexts (i.e., innovate), we have created indirect exchanges via multisided platforms, cryptocurrency, global stock markets, and mortgages that make it appear that trade and exchange do not exist for the everyday person. But they do. French economist Frederick Bastiat stressed that life would not survive without trade. Bastiat argued that without communication language would not exist, and without language humans would be unable to think and contemplate. As a result, human beings would not thrive at all without these basic skills that allow them to relate fully with one another. With the rise of technology, these basic tenets of society have fallen to the background much like a processor chip is rarely seen in a computing device. However, without the processor chip, there is no computation; similarly, without trade, there is no society. Simply put, communication occurs because humans need to be connected to one another. Then, because they are connected to one another, social norms and language develop. These norms and language facilitate the emergence of trade. Thus, examining trade and its role in society can shed light on how human beings are connected and how service ecosystems emerge.

It is helpful to consider value-in-exchange to clarify this position (Vargo and Lusch 2008, 2011, 2016, 2017). Although value generally can refer to a benefit that arises because of trade, value-in-use specifically refers to the particular benefit that is specifically derived from a good or an object when it is drawn upon for use in a particular context. Consider, for example, a tree as a resource. A value-in-use perspective emphasizes the tree and the "value-in-use" that is associated with resources such as "paper" or "lumber" or "table." Basically, the paper, lumber, and table are the tree

ture research on practices can assist with clarifying how or why the
ies of actors commonly develop over time particularly with respect
hnological actors, as well as the doings and actions of said actors. A
ce approach emphasizes the "doings," actions, or activities sanc-
l to help others, or that, in other words, provide service. Over time,
doings (i.e., the activities, practices, or actions enacted to help oth-
an be sanctioned in various ways. Building on the concept of service
stems, it is possible to emphasize how the smaller parts of a service
n give rise to the order parameters that provide order and logic to a
e system (Meynhardt et al. 2016). Emphasizing practices, these
eters can be viewed as emergent from practices, although they have
lly been studied as guided by institutions, or social rules, norms, and
s that guide individual behavior (DiMaggio 1988; Scott 2001). A
ce approach highlights individual behaviors as fundamental to the
f regulations, norms, and beliefs that order and yield logic in a service
n. Simultaneously, it also highlights individual behaviors as funda-
l to the disruption of existing regulations, norms, and beliefs and
ly contributing to the disarray and chaos that can degenerate service
stems. These distinctions vitalize and offer life to some service eco-
ns, while destroying and weakening other service ecosystems. Under
conditions, these behaviors or practices permit service ecosystems to
ere over extensive stretches of time. Mutually associated actors
n associated with each other through these practices; in truth, as they
n associated throughout time, they adjust to each other. As a service
stem develops, actors remain consolidated, in light of the fact that
nay have adjusted their practices to each other.

ke for example that among specific demographics the action of using
tags" is well known. Using a "hashtag" is sometimes favored over a
y explanation because the act of using a hashtag identifies that the
s privy to specialized knowledge and membership in a special group.
ver, among other groups of users, "hashtags" may signal dislike and
e seen as senseless. A researcher for this situation could distinguish
onduct of "using hashtags" and "understanding hashtags" as the
lary or limit of the service ecosystem. In other words, the extent to
practices are perceived positively or negatively can assist researchers
istinguishing the limits of a service ecosystem. The researcher would
e to concentrate on empirically based practices to identify the service
stem by distinguishing the practice that is of significance to the study.

from a value-in-use perspective; each of these is the tree in a manufactured or processed form that is created for a specific context. On the other hand, a value-in-exchange perspective instead would emphasize the age of the tree, or the number of years required for the plant to grow from a seedling to a tree; it would also emphasize the hours spent cutting down the tree and transporting the tree, for example. Moreover, it would also emphasize that, from a value-in-exchange perspective, the number of labor hours worked in order for the consumer to be able to purchase the "lumber" or "table" are part of the equation. Essentially, those "number of hours worked" are exchanged for the "number of years that the plant grew" and for the "hours spent cutting down and transporting the tree." This value-in-exchange perspective emphasizes what we "do" in order to make the trade happen, or what we do in order to interact with others. This highlights the humanity of trade and exchange processes, underscores that which we are truly exchanging when we trade for goods or objects. That is, a value-in-exchange perspective emphasizes that we are essentially trading our skills, knowledge, and expertise in order to gain access to the skills, knowledge, and expertise of others. There has not yet been enough emphasis on understanding how actors do this—how they integrate their own resources in order to trade and exchange. This is an important aspect of service ecosystems because the time affects all actors equally. Time waits for no one, and expires with every second. Time does not discriminate nor can it be allocated according to monetary worth or social capital. Time is a valuable resource that has been underresearched, although it is the currency by which we live our lives. By emphasizing value-in-exchange, the minutes, hours, and days invested into a project or process can be more seriously considered.

Though trade is central to markets, many argue that trade should not be based on pure economic theory and valuation of goods. A more meaningful approach would be to consider trade as a function of relationships and social networks (Achrol 1997). This is because a better understanding of relationships and the ensuing social networks that arise because of trade can offer nuanced insight into how we create value in service ecosystems. Such an understanding would also point outside the dyad of the firm–customer ownership exchanges that have prevailed in much of the organizational theory and business management literature. Much of the criticism regarding the "exchange paradigm" raises issues with that "restricted" view of exchange that is often focused on the dyadic trade of goods for money, and has limited the views on how the context of exchange frames specific times and places (Bagozzi 1975). A high-level extended view of the macro environment that surrounds trade and exchange puts into perspective how context influences trade (Akaka et al. 2013; Chandler and Vargo 2011). Historic perspectives of trade offer broad holistic approaches for thinking about how exchange enables society as a whole (e.g., Bastiat 1860). A service-ecosystem approach extends these views by considering service—the application of resources for the benefit of others—and its implicit interplay with exchange.

In this chapter, literature on practices, engagement, and service systems are incorporated to create a comprehensive perspective on innovation as a way of connecting actors together. These topics have yet to be linked to each other, although each topic has a broad and versatile theoretical structure. This chapter presents the case that incorporation of these differing sources of literature can aid scholars and theorists in clarifying the modern circumstances that have materialized new ways of engaging social technological actors.

To adopt a holistic perspective on the emergence of technological actors, these various literature streams help to develop how we can discuss the service ecosystem at various magnifications such as the micro, meso, and macro magnifications (Chandler et al. 2018). Oscillating the focus can help, for instance, to better understand how interactive texting programs can be substituted for customer service representatives. At a micro magnification, cellular devices (texting) and Automated Teller Machines (ATMs) replace human bank tellers, which is changing everyday behaviors and actions. It is no longer necessary to drive or walk to a financial institution every day in order to withdraw cash to trade. These behaviors have been replaced by electronic funds transfers and credit cards that bypass the physical visit to a financial institution. Aside from removing the human behaviors related to social interactions during the service experience, the introduction of these technological actors, along with others, are a central force that is changing society as a service ecosystem. At a meso magnification, this looks like a multisided platform such as an SMS texting service or an ATM security service attracting financial institutions to their service platform since financial institutions rarely have the technological skills, know-how, or competences to successfully operate technological actors and multisided platforms. In essence, financial institutions outsource this service by joining these platforms. In order to harness the value of these affiliations, they invite, encourage, and, in some cases, require their own customers to also join these multisided platforms. In this way, the

multisided platform congeals a specific context that
the rules, norms, and profit orientation of the fin
affiliations among financial institutions, their cus
sided platforms then evolve into contexts that are
financial institutions. Consumers, or humans, are
writing remiss to take the responsibility for securin
actions in electronic spaces, and so they typically d
knowledge of the financial institutions in vettin
macro magnification, this can be viewed as a
emerges based on the values, norms, needs, belie
financial institutions, as well as the values, norms,
tudes of the financial institutions' customers. Toge
mutually participate in evolving the service ecosys
plasticity of the service ecosystem, any changes, e
tions of any element of the service ecosystem woul
the fluidity and stability of the service ecosystem
perspectives focus on viewpoints that highlight
same phenomena due to their immersion within c
they present a more holistic perspective that allows
and dynamics accompanying the social shift tow
actors in the marketplace.

Practices and Engagem

Micro-level perspectives on technological actors c
sion of practices because practices can be credite
technological actors. This micro-level viewpoint f
actor and features the "doings" and activities
obvious to scientists. Practices are commonly n
study than both engagement and service system
defined as and limited to actions that are funda
investigation. The ongoing study of service system
tions already exist among actors and that service s
It has been demanding to empirically study servi
consistently possible to recognize the limits of sys
this supposition. It is frequently difficult to dicta
and where it ends. It may very well be productiv
centrate their investigations on practices, then
over time.

This involves looking from a miniaturized scale level point of view at the marvels of significance.

However, researchers commonly attribute their own meaning to what which they can observe; in this instance, the action, or practice, then becomes a different level of importance. As a result, researchers must be quick minded and aware with respect to their own incentives and achievements with the research. Most practice theorists hone in on human activity. Meanwhile, others are concerned only with human activity that is willful or intentional. Ortner (1984) takes this a step in the other direction by describing how actors inadvertently influence their surroundings without intention, simply by going about their daily lives. For instance, the practice of flying to faraway destinations produces significant carbon footprints that are detrimental to the actor's surroundings and therefore impacts the actor's environment without the conscious decision to do so. By only "doing," this actor impacts his or her environment. In another circumstance, some actors who are newly graduated from university often improve their local economy, due their achievement of college degrees and work offerings. For this reason, some researchers argue that practices also include mental and emotional aspects of a social activity (Schatzki 1996). This comprises, for instance, a smile, which generally represents friendliness or support. Or, it can consist of a smirk, which usually advocates silliness or fun. Again, what is observed needs to be associated with the cognitive and affective dimensions of the social behavior.

Because different researchers think about "practices" from varying theoretical perspectives, a seamless amelioration of service and practice concepts has not yet been presented (Brauchler and Postill 2010). This has been an obstacle for researchers to overcome. Generally speaking, practice refers to sets of regularized activities and actions (Schatzki et al. 2001). It has also been shown that a practice also can include the understanding and alignment of social action (Schau et al. 2009). This can incorporate, for instance, an unspoken agreement to leave a dinner before 11 pm. In this situation, an observer may recognize that immediately around 9 pm a group of practices will begin to take place and the dinner would become empty. This can happen without coordination or direct communication, and highlights how social action is implicitly coordinated and aligned. This is important in service ecosystems because much of this occurs without direct interaction.

Sometimes practices vary. Varying practices can become immersed in certain service ecosystems once they become aligned. In these instances, they may be consequential or complementary. In some situations, institutions or "regulative, normative and cultural-cognitive elements that, together with associated activities and resources" confirm the acceptance or legitimacy of certain practices and ultimately stabilize service ecosystems (Scott 2001, p. 48). When there are stable institutions, these practices are dominant in a service ecosystem, and this helps the service ecosystem to retain form and persist into the future (Chandler et al. 2018). However, some practices may appear abnormal or deviant; they may vary from other practices. Misalignment of a service ecosystem can be caused by the creation of institutional dissonance. In these cases, service-ecosystem alignment is difficult to achieve because of competing institutions giving rise to diverse or conflicting behaviors or practices (Gehman et al. 2012). When practices are not aligned, the service ecosystem may deteriorate or can become institutionally dissonant which leads to service ecosystems falling out of form (Chandler et al. 2018). Because the service ecosystem cannot maintain form, practices may dominate one another or clash with each other. In this way, in certain circumstances, service ecosystems center around specific practices.

Sometimes a practice roots the service ecosystem in a specific way of "doing" or in a system of actions that are unique to the context in which the practice is embedded. Firms are typically perceived as the overarching authority on practices in the conventional service research literature. That is, the firm has generally been seen as the actor that decides how practices are imposed in the marketplace. For instance, the corporation may presume that peanut butter and jelly go together and therefore produce bundles of peanut butter and jelly to be sold at grocery stores. It is assumed that firms put practices into action in the marketplace and that consumers then adjust these practices to themselves. However, scholars have exhibited that corporations are often unable to command or effect all practices on their own. Sometimes, the alignment or misalignment of practices among actors cannot be controlled by corporations. This frequently happens in healthcare scenarios, and can sometimes occur in fitness scenarios.

Due to the number of incessant triggers in the external environment of a service ecosystem, practices constantly evolve. Appropriately, some practices become aligned toward particular service systems. Although service ecosystems have been studied as "relatively self-contained, self-adjusting systems of resource-integrating actors connected by shared institutional arrangements and mutual value creation through service exchange," practices can be nuanced and customized for specific contexts (Vargo and Lusch (2016, p. 10/11). The service-ecosystem viewpoint highlights institutions as the glue keeping actors together, which results in change and dynamics occurring across jointly linked actors. More specifically, service ecosystems frequently change in unforeseeable ways as a result of possible misalignment or isolation by all actors. Essentially, practices serve as a means for change in service systems because they are the first area in a service system that adjusts to external changes. Rather than stressing boundaries, a service-ecosystem viewpoint highlights change by way of institutions.

For instance, healthcare clients may not heed the recommendations of their doctor, and, similarly, fitness clients may not heed the advice of their personal trainers. Likewise, products may not be utilized in methods originally proposed for by firms, or products may be altered by consumers after purchase. McColl-Kennedy et al. (2012) find that practice styles influence service ecosystems because non-firm actors such as consumers adapt practices to fit their own needs and wants, and shape them to what they feel and think. They present that a practice style is customization of a practice to fit a context in a way that organizes the service system to achieve a specific value creation effort. In this way, practice styles are customized practices in a specific context, in a specific service ecosystem. Practice styles become the transition points upon which service ecosystems continually change. Practice styles result in the order of relations, actors, materials, and activity around a particular value creation effort. Because a trigger or new event may change some aspect of the external environment, changes in practice styles are often unavoidable and typically catalyze evolution in the service ecosystem. This cycle repeats indefinitely.

Meanwhile, engagement is also key for thinking about how actors interact with each other. Engagement can appear to be a corporation that is forwarding emails to customers who have registered for their mailing list, or a loyal customer who has been attending the same restaurant for many years. Engagement is multifaceted and complex. Schaufeli and Baker (2004) and Schaufeli et al. (2002) described engagement as channeling energy into tasks. Csikszentmihalyi (1997) popularized engagement as a psychological state that occurs when one's knowledge and skills become fully engaged when one attempts to overcome a reasonable challenge. On the other hand, Kahn (1990, 1992) relates engagement to being fully present in the moment. These studies propose engagement as being continuous over time. Engagement is also relational in that actors take on social roles that spawn connections joining actors to one another (Akaka and Chandler 2011). These relational links are the ties that put actors together as families, markets, or communities. Engagement is also a strenuous disparate subject to define because it is often mistaken with other concepts. Engagement is a fundamental concept that transcends disciplines. Although it has been studied in education and learning (Pascarella and Terenzini 1991; Kearsley and Shneiderman 1998), it received significant scholarly attention in the psychology and management literature.

The study of engagement became a focus of service research when Brodie et al. (2011) proposed customer engagement as a psychological state induced by service experiences and connections. They declare that this state constantly evolves over time as a result of situational conditions. Other scholars affirm this conceptualization, proposing that engagement is a set of deep and meaningful connections that are dynamic and experiential (Calder and Malthouse 2008; Malthouse and Calder 2011; Bolton 2011). This again points to a psychological nature of engagement. Building on these foundations, Chandler and Lusch (2015) elaborated engagement from a systems perspective. They desired to account for the impact of connections on the framing of psychological states, which they presented as dispositions. Appropriately, they outline five properties of engagement. These five properties are either external (i.e., connections) or internal to an actor (i.e., dispositions). The connections of an actor surface over time (temporal connections) and relational space (relational connections). They are formed from exchanges of the past giving rise to concurrent actors.

Combining practices and engagement, it is important to recognize that the effect of the two is best viewed with a meso-level lens. Practices are simply the actions of an individual. However, when exploring a situation, a meso magnification that combines both practices and engagement can help to clarify the emergent role of technological actors in the marketplace. Whether human or inhuman, alternatively, engagement stems from existing ties between and among actors that are a consequence of a practice. Once a practice happened, engagement could remain. That is, practices—or sayings and doings—are the actions that initially link actors together; after the practice has been completed, engagement prevails over time.

Combining practices and engagement is particularly critical to clarifying how technological actors might alter the marketplace. To better understand this, Chandler and Lusch (2015) assert a systemic perspective on engagement, such that engagement manifests partly through temporal connections and relational connections. Differing parts of engagement are dispositions, psychological, or proclivity states of an actor. These can be aligned toward accomplishing a unique future, accommodating a unique past, or discovering importance in a unique present. The *temporal connections* and *relational connections* are neutral on their own but can be pointed out and utilized by an actor, according to the actor's dispositions. This is particularly significant when it comes to technological actors because technological actors are generally extracted on an actor's dispositions.

For these reasons, value propositions promote interaction by appealing to the dispositions of an individual. If value ideas are successful, they tie together service structures because they often lead to engagement. Value propositions convey solutions that bring together practices (Gummesson 2008; Payne et al. 2008). Chandler and Lusch (2015) propose value propositions as invitations from actors to one another. Technological actors should be regarded as value propositions in this way because they can deliver different ways of interaction. As a result, actors will react favorably to just a few of these engagements. In fact, value ideas are more or less persuasive to multiple stakeholders, whether they are consumers, manufacturers, sellers, or otherwise. S-D logic and its related service-ecosystem view focuses on service, rather than goods and money, as the hidden engine of value creation (Vargo and Lusch 2004a, 2008, 2011, 2016). This perspective stresses a value-in-exchange approach to shared value or co-creation, which illustrates how actors (e.g., companies and customers) incorporate services together to generate value for themselves and for others. In fact, neither businesses nor customers have all the resources they need to thrive. Therefore sharing, helping one another, and engaging with one another is necessary in order to survive. Bastiat drew on prior work by Adam Smith (1776) to direct attention to the division of labor and how it facilitates wealth creation. However, Bastiat also added that it is not only human labor which creates value, but also the natural elements from which human beings can draw in the world. Meanwhile, Smith built upon the division of specialist expertise that had been debated since Plato's time to create the basis behind his claim that splitting labor would inevitably maximize a company and/or nation's market efficiency and income. Smith claims that division labor would yield the great improvements in national wealth since this would lead to specialists who are the best in a particular topic. Smith also recognized, however, that specialization would increase restrictions on individual access to required resources. Thus, without trade and exchange, the right of a person to access others' resources would ultimately depend on the merit of his work. In this respect, increased specialization is positively linked to increased dependency on others, and hence, by developing specialized skills, the reliance of an individual on others decreases. This way of thinking has informed macro-level values, trends, beliefs, and attitudes.

However, this rationale underlying the division of labor in most Westernized countries has culminated in the identification of types of activity that were both productive and unproductive. In short, Smith laid a basis for thinking of value-in-use as a "true" value, while value-in-exchange became thought of as a "nominal" value. Smith goes on to argue that country wealth depends on the output of tangible goods, which ultimately led to the idea of exportable products that could contribute to national wealth (Vargo and Lusch 2004a). It is important to note that Bastiat's (1860) views somewhat diverged from those of Smith (1776). More specifically, Bastiat focuses on activities as fundamental to exchange and argued that value is not found in tangible products per se. He says that value is dependent on the benefit of activities regardless of whether goods or objects are exchanged. Those activities, performed in concert with the activities of others, create value. In this way, interdependence is requisite for a successful division of labor. Many early scholars yielded to economic pressures and philosophy and preferred Smith's view of productive labor that focused on the output of tangible resources. The firm's emphasis on tangible goods production thus prevailed over time.

By focusing on engagement, the proposed perspective aligns more closely with that of Bastiat that articulated value as the ensuing relationship that exists after services have been exchanged. Because of the paradigmatic emphasis on the exchange of goods, service has been viewed as difficult to exchange because it does not often involve ownership (Parasuraman et al. 1985). Service was seen as a fleeting action that dissipated the moment it was initiated, which makes it difficult to manage. Moreover, it is typically difficult to train and organize employees for service because each service experience is unique. These ideas have frustrated managers for years and subsequently invigorated exploration of how service can lead to value creation among actors who are not typically connected to one another. Ultimately, this led to a broader reconceptualization of service and exchange systems (Chandler and Vargo 2011; Akaka et al. 2013). This included questioning exchange from a high level including what is being exchanged, why it is being exchanged, and how value is co-created because of exchange; conversely, this also means question why exchange does not happen or why particular goods or services are not exchanged, and the destruction of value (Akaka and Vargo 2015). Essentially, a renewed perspective now highlights service as the application of knowledge and skills for the benefit of others (Vargo and Lusch 2004b). This perspective highlights value-in-exchange and the interdependence that is fundamental to the spirit of Bastiat's philosophy. Moreover, it reveals the overlooked ways that customers participate in value creation (Prahalad and Ramaswamy 2004). It also reintroduced the idea that consumers have always been interested in value co-creation, and that without consumer or product interaction, businesses alone cannot generate value.

Throughout a business environment, key sharing elements appear. To identify the components of exchange within service ecosystems, it is helpful to revisit the five axioms of S-D logic (Vargo and Lusch 2017). Rather than focusing on exchange as sacrifice for benefit, it is important to view trade and exchange as bringing actors together. Axiom 1 says "Service is the fundamental foundation of exchange." Service is characterized as the "use of services for the benefit of another" within S-D logic. Service is the center of exchange. This description suggests that service is a method for getting people together, since one agent (e.g., individual or organization) has something that would help another. Nonetheless, at the same time service is only useful where there is a shortage of resources. In other words, a beneficiary is only that if anything of worth is offered up by the beneficiary to obtain anything with a more valued worth. Access to natural capital, though, is a significant consideration in the willingness even to offer service. Natural resources are distributed unevenly across the globe. For those who have access to unique natural resources should always have relevant expertise and competencies. As a consequence, specialization in expertise determines the division of labor, although this is at least partly related to the location and availability of natural (and other) resources.

Axiom 2 asserts that value is co-created by multiple actors, often including the beneficiary. S-D logic differs from traditional notions of value creation, which focus on firms as value creators (e.g., Porter 1985). Within a business environment, many players, including the recipient, often co-create the benefit. This points to the importance of networks of relationships, because a focus on the dyad in exchange, even value co-creation, can be misleading (Akaka et al. 2012; Chandler and Vargo 2011). A service-ecosystem perspective reflects a network structure established by division of labor, which requires different actors to take on different roles to establish and maintain their relationships (Akaka and Chandler 2011). Considering dyadic exchange without knowing its position in a wider sense does not explain how the dyadic exchange is placed in an expanded social or cultural environment and effects it has on the wider macro environment. Taking a network perspective provides insights into how multiple actors form distinct relationships and how resources are allocated and exchanged across multiple relationships (Akaka et al. 2012).

All types of actors are resource integrators, as asserted by Axiom 3. The perspective of resource integrators of both social and economic players sheds light on the notion that all actors are capable of engaging in value creation and that trade is motivated by multisided views on value. Resource sharing therefore unites people as each actor has specific needs and depends on a multitude of other actors with different resources to fulfill those needs. On the other side, each actor will theoretically combine their own resources in order to also support other actors or participate in value creation. Therefore, resource integration not only unites actors but also divides operational resources among them as they combine capital to generate value for themselves and others. Traditionally, it has been established that goods are at the core of value production and trade. The priority given to operational capital by S-D reasoning suggests that awareness and expertise are key drivers of getting people together. Many times the information and expertise are concealed within a vast network of objects and intermediaries and people take for granted the knowledge required for making a meal or running a university, for instance. This is because sharing is based on someone else's desire for expertise and skills. In certain cases, it is apparent that individual actors require access to other people's expertise and skills, for example when an organization requires the services of a certified public accountant.

Service is essentially a process that incorporates others sharing their knowledge and competences with others. Based on their participation in the process and their unique modes of resource integration, access to resources begins to look more appealing than ownership of physical resources. This is an important consideration because traditional economic models emphasize resource ownership as a central means to wealth creation. However, for this wealth model the focus on service and joint participation in service processes raises essentially issues that challenge the prevailing paradigm. In particular, it is difficult to determine how wealth accumulates based on joint participation in important processes, or when information is applied as the basis for value formation, for example.

Axiom 4 assigns the eye of the value beholder to the beneficiary of the service. Phenomenological significance is also analyzed via the prism of practice. Because no human can experience the benefits or sufferings of another human, it is almost impossible for all humans to understand the valuation processes of other humans. In other words, value is unique to each person. Nevertheless, despite the personal insight and knowledge that each person has, most actors will support most other actors. In other words, many actors empathize with others, and thus feel it is beneficial to plan for and create new ideas and new solutions that can address particular needs. Many times, multiple actors come to agree on a new idea or solution. While value may be calculated and assessed from different viewpoints at particular points in time, overall value is subject to change over time and space. Together, actors can evolve a new or solution. Since all actors communicate constantly with one another in order to consider and fulfill unmet desires and needs, they contribute to the renovation of connections that looks like innovation. In other words, because meaning is special and phenomenological, participants need to communicate constantly to better understand evolving preferences and establish appropriate solutions or value propositions. This need to consider diverse perceptions on value often represents a need to diversify labor, so that similar approaches will fulfill several different needs or desires. For certain cases, those who are in need and unwilling to pursue a market-based alternative will become the service suppliers for themselves and those with specific needs (i.e., entrepreneurs). Sometimes, this cultivates innovation.

Axiom 5 notes that institutions drive many of the considerations discussed in the previous axioms. Institutions are rules and social norms which form how people communicate and behave. Institutional structures are arrays of entities that interact in a single geographical, social, and cultural sense and affect how decisions and judgments are produced. The embeddedness of an economy within a society represents the centrality of organizations in trade and value formation. However, organizations have not traditionally been tasked with considering how communication and language shape how trade commences. Instead, organizations are oriented toward profit maximization and have been considered to be separate from the social tapestry that permeates society. Without an idea of their true impact on society and how to communicate with others actors, organizations are single-purposed to amass the wealth and capital that leads to shareholder value. Increasingly in modern society, however, organizations are being seen as actors that indeed influence institutions inasmuch as regular humans and actors can also be seen as active participants in value creation. Although one single actor can initiate a new idea or innovation, no single actor can bring that wish, desire, or idea to fruition alone. In order for the new idea to become a solution for larger issues in the service ecosystem, other actors need to be engaged. Those new ideas or institutions are needed for actors to enact practices that contribute to value creation for individuals as well as collectives (Warde 2005; Kjellberg and Helgesson 2007; Schau et al. 2009). Institutions thereby draw people together and allow them to engage with each other by having a shared sense of how to act and communicate. Institutions, however, can impose limits for what forms of work in which different people can or cannot participate. It is also important to consider the context within which the trade takes place and appreciate the reasons for trade and the impacts of exchange in developing culture.

To understand the antecedents and implications of trade, attention must be given to the sense of trade that makes and motivates interaction. Extended sociohistorical systems influence trade choices or the various transaction forms, modes of mutual and financial exchange, the agreements on shared benefits. Most humans rely upon contextual cues to make choices like these and most often mindlessly participate in meaning formation at any given moment. When actors continually influence one another in these ways, they are offering value propositions to one another (Chandler and Lusch 2015). When an invitation or new idea is accepted, the trajectory of the entire service ecosystem is altered. For example, when a miner unearths a mineral, it is typically because the mineral will be crafted into a piece of jewelry. Based on the socioeconomic history of this context, the miner uses his or her resources to help someone else—even though the value does not appear for several days, months, or even years. In this way, the service has already begun at the moment of unearthing, although the service trajectory transpires over time and distance interweaving many more actors into the service experience until an actual trade occurs. This grand exchange clearly exists: no matter how micro an exchange between two people is, it is also macro in the sense that these two people that constitute an exchange between two (or more) separate countries. However, when an innovation or value proposition is introduced into the grand interaction, the trajectory of the entire service experience might be altered, either slightly or greatly. For example, maybe there is an opportunity send the mineral to a local artisan who makes jewelry for Etsy instead of to the corporate jeweler whose goods sell at Costco. In this case, the entire service trajectory shifts for all those involved and all the connections are essentially renovated. Furthermore, the future of the service ecosystem is altered accordingly. Similarly, when a salesperson trades micro-level with a customer, two companies simultaneously trade at the macro level. In turn, the trade of a given resource can occur over and over again as it passes through a multitude of intermediaries because several micro-encounters may collectively generate a meso- or macro-value amount (e.g., national wealth).

Early conceptualizations of value thus depend on the commitment invested into a good or service by a corporation and harvested by a customer at a given time and location. This suggests that value in a service environment arises from the experience of the service within a phenomenological context that is unique to the service beneficiary. In other words, the value of the service depends on the particular interactions and context of the beneficiary, including the larger macro values, norms, beliefs, and culture that influence the beneficiary. As such, value emerges from the multitudes of exchange that mature at a specific moment in time (Chandler and Lusch 2015). Because of this, trade should be perceived as more than just a buy-and-sell economic transaction, and it is more than a social interaction between two individuals. Alternatively, each trade should be viewed as a moment of transition within a continuous, eternal, omnipresent sharing of commodities used for the good of others. When one simple trade changes, there is a wider effect in the macro environment of the service ecosystem.

Because communication is micro and momentary as well as grand and omnipresent, it is always invisible to track. Those micro instants of interaction deposit effects into the macro level, thereby giving trade and exchange some form and function. Chandler and Vargo (2011) describe this by proposing context as a way to study and frame exchange at different analytic levels of relationships: the micro, meso and macro levels. These magnifications occur only in researchers' minds; in fact, they are clustered within each other, with the micro-or smallest-level contained in the meso and macro levels. They are neither set nor mutually exclusive. As Chandler and Vargo (2011) explain, "By defining context as a unique set of actors and the unique reciprocal links among them, it is possible to see how hundreds of actors and links may constitute one specific context, while two actors and links may constitute another context (page 41)." We may think of a service environment as the water in a broad bucket; it could be appropriate to examine various measurements of this water to answer a study problem. The micro level, for example, is like taking a tablespoon of this water for study, while the meso level is like taking a cup of the same water and the macro level is like taking a gallon of that water. The water teaspoon is inside the cup of water which is inside the gallon of water. They are different from each other but they are still the same somehow.

While such several, nested levels are relational representations of the grand interaction, it is necessary to remember that certain levels are intertwined technically. Exchange therefore occurs at each level, but at each level may reverberate differently, similar to how the salinity of water can vary in a drop, cup, or gallon of the same water sample. When one of these is renovated, so are the others. In this way, trade can vary over time and space—for example, it can be put together by more or similar players whose roles may be distinguished differently. Likewise, water can change its shape over time: it can appear as a fluid (i.e., steam) or solid (i.e., ice) under various conditions. Context similarly can be expressed in these ways—it gives trade structure and dimension as limited by its socioeconomic history. However, innovation and value propositions serve as a catalyst for renovating this socioeconomic history. In this way, interaction and trade can be viewed from an actor's particular viewpoint in several respects. As meaning lies in a researcher's mind, it can be used to shed light on any fascinating phenomena. It is highly important when analyzing meaning as a phenomenological emergence; context should be used to interpret the interaction as it occurs from the focal actor's perspective. Innovation and value propositions, as they are evaluated, accepted, or rejected, renovate context as well.

Particular service contexts have been studied to identify particular modes of exchange through which different actors with specialized skills apply their competences for the benefit of others (Akaka and Vargo 2015). It is in these contexts where experiences emerge and are evaluated and value is co-created. Drawing on the structure of context (Chandler and Vargo 2011) and the components of exchange (Vargo and Lusch 2017) discussed above, we reframe more traditional views on service encounters and servicescapes by considering the broader service ecosystem within which other service contexts are embedded. This is important because it helps to explain why innovation occurs simultaneously at many levels and is such a complex phenomenon.

Context frames exchange at micro level by boundary exchange as it occurs among individual actors. A direct exchange between two actors is a simplistic exchange between the lowest number of individual actors. And the context surrounding the interaction in this case is a dyad. Service interactions are also examined by analyzing particular positions that human participants play to participate in interaction and/or create meaning. In other words, micro-level experiences are driven by clear participation criteria and whether or not those criteria are achieved or surpassed dramatically impacts the interest generated in a given interaction or transaction. Work on early services identified a business experience as a key analytical unit for the analysis of value development and trade. In general, a "service encounter is a dyadic interaction between a customer and a service provider" (Surprenant and Solomon 1987, p. 87). Under this service sense, reliability is usually measured by satisfaction (or dissatisfaction) with a given experience. Service experiences may be called a micro-level sense of operation, since they call attention to human actions and relationships within a dyad. Bitner (1990) asserts that the dyad occurs from a customer perspective; however, in actuality, many different actors beyond the dyad are involved in creating a service experience. However, if service is treated as the cornerstone of all trade, then only goods-mediated transactions may be called a service experience. It applies the meaning of the service to the skilled work necessary to deliver a service and the phenomenological assessment of an interaction. In other words, a service experience will frame any transaction instance at micro level or dyad during a co-creation cycle of a given interest. Nevertheless, since short-term outcomes, such as customer loyalty, result in long-term results, such as partnerships between firm and client, such experiences cannot be treated in isolation. Individual gatherings, as well as their collectives, should be viewed within the broader organization context within which they take place.

Zooming out, the attention of a researcher moves to the context where frames interact between dyads at the meso level. Exchange brokered—or indirect—is mediated by an entity who is specific to, or positioned within, two dyads. The specific participant of one dyad represents one actor, as does the other actor in the other dyad. As Chandler and Vargo (2011) explain, "two actors indirectly serve one another by serving the same actor (p. 41)." Therefore the context around trade is a triad. This meso level of trade will theoretically lead to differing opinions on valuation as it requires multiple viewpoints. It is necessary to consider the different perspectives that lead to value formation at this level of interaction—some views overlap while others diverge. Through widening the exchange spectrum beyond the dyad, we may find increasing degrees of sophistication in the formation and distribution of values. The conceptualization of servicescape started when Bitner recognized the need to consider the "environment-user" relationship that framed the firm–customer encounter. In addition, social surroundings were considered as influential on exchange, and this included social environments restricted to a particular time and place (Johnstone 2012; Tombs and McColl-Kennedy 2010) as well as extended social contexts (Nilsson and Ballantyne 2014). Servicescapes were considered to be artificially created as a culmination of corporate strategies intertwined by customer feedback (Arnould et al. 1998). Early discussions of servicescapes focused on human-made, physical aspects of exchange environments, but eventually extended to include symbolic and natural elements as well (Rosenbaum and Massiah 2011). However, if we consider the importance of natural resources in service and exchange (Bastiat 1860), the servicescape broadens. The use of natural resources within a servicescape contributes to the value of specialization as it applies to resource use and distribution, and calls attention to environmental concerns. When considering how a servicescape might affect customers, this becomes an issue of public health and corporate social responsibility. It has been shown that nature and individual natural elements can heal and restore humans. This suggests the need to conceptualize servicescapes beyond a single time and space occurrence and find an extended macro-level social and cultural framework that shares frames.

Context frames interchange at the macro level by bounding it, since it occurs within triads. Usually, multiple players are involved, and the framework of macro-level trading is a network of transactions. This network of exchanges is linked not only by various actors and ties, but also by a variety of organizations and cultures. The macro level doesn't generally reflect a regional or global view. This is a perspective that encompasses micro and meso interactions and accounts for various factors like time and space that lead to value development and trade motives. This is a critical level to understand as macro-level relationships at micro and meso levels can have serious and long-lasting impacts on demand and value development.

Macro-level approaches to exchange can be found in the work regarding service science and service systems (e.g., Maglio and Spohrer 2008). The study of service systems provides a context of exchange that includes interactions among people, technology, and organizations. According to Maglio et al., a service system is "a dynamic value-cocreation configuration of resources, including people, organizations, shared information (language, laws, measures, methods), and technology, all connected internally and externally to other service systems by value propositions." In this way, service systems can be identified at micro, meso, and macro levels of action and interaction, because they frame individual actions within broader dyadic interactions and even broader networks of relationships (Vargo et al. 2008). Business frameworks, however, need a macro-level viewpoint because it draws attention to people's and infrastructure networks, and how diverse services are combined to generate value within.

A machine view at the macro level helps frame interactions beyond a dyadic experience and even a wider operation sequence. In addition to natural resources, service systems include the integration of various technologies and the means by which they are created (i.e., innovation) (Maglio and Spohrer 2008). In other words, service networks offer insight not only into how trading takes place but also how new partnerships of trade are created. Of this cause, a perception of trade on macro-level utility networks stresses creativity and co-creation, and new sources of interest. The creativity cycle is better approached at a macro perspective, since it needs to be analyzed over extended time and space. Nevertheless, the evaluation of various layers of research from a business environment viewpoint is required to understand how new innovations arise, develop, and propagate through different service structures.

The meta-layer is time and space; it is the temporality that stretches a network's static view to a fluid view of a service system and enables connections to be analyzed across distinct service systems. The temporality and expanded scope is where trade reverberations occur and take hold. The meta-layer is not a category as it transcends micro, meso and macro levels and helps researchers to understand multi- and sublevel connections. Studying one degree in contrast from the others prevents a true comprehension of any economic or social phenomena.

A service-ecosystem perspective aligns with prior discussions on service systems and a systemic view of value creation and exchange. Importantly, however, a service-ecosystem perspective demands that these different layers of measurement be collectively considered and how distinct service structures interact. Different conceptual rates are interconnected by structures or social norms that direct human behavior and interaction. By the specific implementation of procedures or the code of conduct for a single business experience, such organizations may be analyzed on a micro basis. Institutions can also be assessed at a meso-level servicescape such as the formal and informal rules that guide interaction with a brand (Schau et al. 2009). At a macro-level point of view, organizations can be regarded as underlying social norms and cultural concepts that lay out wider modes of interpretation and connectivity, such as language and technology, that enable service networks to interact. Thus, the meta-layer in a service ecosystem is interwoven across different analysis levels (Chandler and Vargo 2011).

Service systems are important as they are useful in understanding how different actors respond to each other, be they computers, human beings, or businesses. A focus on service networks provides a macro-level viewpoint as it casts a broader eye on the focal phenomenon. Several examples of service systems include the set of restaurant workers involved in delivering a cup of coffee to a customer, the set of customers who meet to discuss their favorite brands, or the set of companies involved in a smartphone's supply chain. Each of these represents "value-co-creation configurations of people, technology, value propositions connecting internal and external service systems, and shared information (e.g., language, laws, measures, and methods)" (Maglio and Spohrer 2008, p. 18). In service systems, service structures may consist of people groups, technology, value recommendations, and shared knowledge. These can involve an ATM machine, a sales channel or an enterprise community. These are all value configurations of people, technology, value propositions, and shared information. More generally, scholars have also proposed service systems as "tightly coupled wholes" (Nenonen et al. 2014, p. 10) while others view service systems as smaller subsets of connections (Meynhardt et al. 2016). It is important to note that these are often embedded within vast seas of yet other constellations and universes.

Studying service networks has traditionally been difficult, as they are transient and invisible. Also, they are hard to describe as explicit from each other; that is, the points that delineate one system from another are fuzzy and vague. For this reason, better integration of the literature of practices and interaction with that of service structures will explain how technological actors can renovate the socioeconomic histories of a service ecosystem. If technology actors' practices are synchronized, complementary or both, it can be argued that such practices tie actors together in the same service ecosystem. As they are embedded together for a longer period of time, they come to share the same socioeconomic history. In this way, bits and pieces of the service ecosystem eventually adapt to the technology actors. Technology actors can be of great value to society because they force the service ecosystem to adapt. In addition, actors can remain linked to each other via engagement until the practices expire or are complete. This is important to remember because a significant number of humans keep in contact with technical actors rather than with other humans. The connections are renovated each time a new innovation or value proposition emerges.

Four principles guide researchers to suitable starting points in their investigations of technical actors by reinterpreting service structures as collections of activities that are bound over time. Actors vary in their ability to respond to others and in their social capability. Moreover, social capacity includes all the dimensions in which actors will be able to interact with each other; social capacity includes all the behaviors, acts, and sayings that bind actors to each other. Although the idea of interaction is wider and more inclusive than procedures, both are important for the understanding of service structures. Engagement helps the participants to participate in service systems; activities are simply acts without engagement. Practices meanwhile emerge from interaction. Practices include motive, attitude, or perception of a transpiring behavior. Engagement can increase or decrease the social ability of service structures as it affects how actors interact with each other. The relationship is often constant and momentarily permanent. It ebbs and flows in the service ecosystem, in reaction to the climate. It is important to understand how ecosystems are linked to activities, interaction, and service in order to better understand the technical actors.

Human interdependence promotes trust and co-creation by generating access to essential services and influencing economies and markets alike. This may be called a trade. Since trade or interdependent underpinnings of social institutions can be difficult to see under the intricacies of economic culture, the study of service has been overlooked. Increased processing and distribution of commodities, as well as an emphasis on transaction-based (rather than barter) systems, has diverted researchers from unraveling the central nature of trade. S-D theory has illustrated the role of service in value formation, while stressing the concept of service or applicable services as the basis for trade. However, a deeper understanding of trade within society is required to further grasp the nature of trade in service environments.

The advent and growth of economic theory relied heavily on Smith's understanding of the division of labor and his theories on production based on commodities. The lack of exposure to the service-centered economic theories of Bastiat eventually resulted in a dominant perception of the trade and value formation of the goods. Therefore, while Smith stressed the manufacturing of products, and Bastiat stressed the quality of operation, each concentrated on the nominal or relative value discovered by trade. This emphasis on nominal value measurements as a trade product has restricted knowledge of how value is produced and the reasons behind why trading takes place. The recent resurgence of attention to "service as the basis of all exchange" (Vargo and Lusch 2004a) has necessitated a scholarly move toward explication of service-centered components of exchange and the complexities of the context within which value is co-created.

Although Bastiat (1860) spent a considerable amount of time discussing the social implications of exchange, his ideas remained in the shadows of Adam Smith's (1776) earlier views on national wealth and surplus production. Smith claimed in particular that the division of labor allowed humans to learn different skills in order to manufacture vast amounts of products more effectively so as to prepare for trade. Smith's perspective on national wealth and production was widely accepted and more beneficial for those attempting to develop economic science centered on a microeconomic view (Arndt 1983; Vargo et al. 2006). Thus, Smith's views, which focused mostly on the efficiency of the division of human labor, ultimately provided the foundation for thinking about and strategically developing or managing economic exchange (Vargo et al. 2008).

Framing communication through a service environment viewpoint involves awareness of how experiences through participant and technology networks affect behavior, but also emphasizes the importance of sociohistoric frameworks that direct engagement and value determination. This expanded service context frames communication across various theoretical layers and differing opinions on interest. This approach offers a deeper, more complex trade conceptualization than the microeconomic perspectives that remain dominant market disciplines. An exchange view of the service ecosystem involves an extended view of the context which frames interaction and co-creation of value. In service networks, in particular, various layers of engagement and structures, or hierarchical frameworks, reframe human information and skills within a diverse and fluid exchange network. The S-D philosophy and a business-ecosystem viewpoint draw attention to service—the usage of services for the good of others—as the cornerstone of all trade. An emphasis on organizations allows researchers to analyze and compare similar service elements through various rates of analysis. Oscillating across micro, meso, and macro stages offers a more holistic view of the reasons for getting individuals together and the distribution of labor (i.e., exchange) outcomes. Depending on this, it is possible to consider all trade networks as service networks, all social institutions as service structures, and all markets as service economies.

Future studies should empirically analyze the different elements and communication meanings, and how they contribute to each other. In particular, more analytical research is required that distinguishes between micro, meso, and macro levels and explores the relationships among them. That may lead to a better understanding of the exchange's competitive existence. The conceptual structure also provides a basis for researching how the trade affects co-creation of product and profit. Since co-creation of creativity and meaning are structural processes, taking the viewpoints presented in this chapter will shine a different light on these subjects. Research on the interaction of business environments can also investigate how new technologies influence various components and trade contexts (e.g., interactive market encounters). The philosophical construct discussed above is a first step in reconsidering the role of value production trade as well as the embeddedness of social economies. However, much more work needs to be undertaken to empirically affirm the validity of this process and to grasp more fully the nature and effects of service-for-service trade.

References

Achrol, R.S. 1997. Changes in the Theory of Interorganizational Relations in Marketing: Toward a Network Paradigm. *Journal of the Academy of Marketing Science* 25 (1): 56–71.

Akaka, M.A., and J.D. Chandler. 2011. Roles as Resources: A Social Roles Perspective of Change in Value Networks. *Marketing Theory* 11 (3): 243–260.

Akaka, M.A., and S.L. Vargo. 2015. Extending the Context of Service: From Encounters to Ecosystems. *Journal of Services Marketing* 29 (6/7): 453–462.

Akaka, M.A., S.L. Vargo, and R.F. Lusch. 2012. An Exploration of Networks in Value Cocreation: A Service-Ecosystems View. In *Special Issue–Toward a Better Understanding of the Role of Value in Markets and Marketing*, 13–50. Bingley: Emerald Group Publishing Limited.

———. 2013. The Complexity of Context: A Service Ecosystems Approach for International Marketing. *Journal of International Marketing* 21 (4): 1–20.

Arndt, J. 1983. The Political Economy Paradigm: Foundation for Theory Building in Marketing. *The Journal of Marketing* 47: 44–54.

Arnould, E.J., L.L. Price, and P. Tierney. 1998. Communicative Staging of the Wilderness Servicescape. *Service Industries Journal* 18 (3): 90–115.

Bagozzi, R.P. 1975. Marketing as Exchange. *The Journal of Marketing* 39: 32–39.
Bastiat, F. 1860. *Harmonies of Political Economy*. Vol. 1. London: J. Murray.
Bitner, M.J. 1990. Evaluating Service Encounters: The Effects of Physical Surroundings and Employee Responses. *The Journal of Marketing* 54: 69–82.
Bolton, Ruth N. 2011. Customer Engagement: Opportunities and Challenges for Organizations. *Journal of Service Research* 14 (3): 272–274.
Brauchler, B., and J. Postill. 2010. *Theorising Media and Practice*. Oxford: Berghahn Books.
Brodie, R.J., L.D. Hollebeek, B. Juric, and A. Ilic. 2011. Customer Engagement: Conceptual Domain, Fundamental Propositions, and Implications for Research. *Journal of Service Research* 14 (3): 252–271.
Calder, Bobby J., and Edward C. Malthouse. 2008. Media Engagement and Advertising Effectiveness. In *Kellogg on Advertising and Media*, ed. Bobby J. Calder, 1–36. Hoboken: John Wiley.
Chandler, Jennifer D., and Robert Lusch. 2015. Service Systems: A Broadened Framework and Research Agenda on Value Propositions, Engagement and Service Experience. *Journal of Service Research* 18 (1): 6–22.
Chandler, J.D., and S.L. Vargo. 2011. Contextualization and Value-In-Context: How Context Frames Exchange. *Marketing Theory* 11 (1): 35–49.
Chandler, Jennifer D., Ilias Danatzis, Carolin Wernicke, Melissa Akaka, and David Reynolds. 2018. How Does Innovation Emerge in a Service Ecosystem? *Journal of Service Research*, published online 9/24/2018.
Csikszentmihalyi, Mihaly. 1997. *Finding Flow: The Psychology of Engagement with Everyday Life*. New York: HarperCollins.
DiMaggio, Paul. 1988. Interest and Agency in Institutional Theory. In *Institutional Patterns and Organizations: Culture and Environment*, ed. L.G. Zucker, 3–22. Cambridge, MA: Ballinger.
Gehman, J., L. Trevino, and R. Garud. 2012. Values Work: A Process Study of the Emergence and Performance of Organizational Values Practices. *Academy of Management Journal* 56 (1): 84–112.
Gummesson, Evert. 2008. Extending the Service-Dominant Logic: From Customer Centricity to Balanced Centricity. *Journal of the Academy of Marketing Science* 36 (1): 15–17.
Johnstone, M.L. 2012. The Servicescape: The Social Dimensions of Place. *Journal of Marketing Management* 28 (11–12): 1399–1418.
Kahn, William A. 1990. Psychological Conditions of Personal Engagement and Disengagement at Work. *Academy of Management Journal* 33 (4): 692–724.
———. 1992. To be Fully There: Psychological Presence at Work. *Human Relations* 45 (4): 321–349.
Kearsley, Greg, and Ben Shneiderman. 1998. Engagement Theory: A Framework for Technology-Based Teaching and Learning. *Educational Technology* 38 (5): 20–23.

comfortable and reify our existence. We crave these processes for they give us stability. They strengthen our service ecosystems because our interactions invigorate them. As a result, these processes are difficult to alter because they are hallmarks of our own personal comforts. We created them, we left them there, and we are happy to continue engraving them into the narrative of the human race. These routine behaviors give us comfort and help us to find value and meaning in our everyday lives. They are the basis of service ecosystems and help service ecosystems to retain their form. In the United States and many other Westernized countries, we relish the certainty embedded in these routines and habits. For many human beings, their physical and mental well-being depends on the existence of routine. Because of this, it is certainly possible that the organizations with whom we engage collect, house, and harness data about us and our most personal daily behaviors. To a large extent, many of us enjoy how these data help our favorite organizations like Google or Apple make our lives easier; this occurs when smart devices automatically turn on lights in our houses or when our smart phones give us turn-by-turn directions as we drive to work. All the while, organizations are collecting data about our everyday lives. Many Americans and citizens of other countries are happy to share their data with companies in order to reap the value of autonomous integrations that help us to lead harmonized, simpler lives. The value, again, stems from the predictability of our behaviors, routines, and processes.

When we as individuals reach out to those in our immediate contexts to consider our ideas and value propositions, we engage others in our own attempts to remedy the issues that we have identified in our context. Others may not perceive those situations as issues, and, at times, we may work inadvertently against one another in trying to solve a problem. In the end, we each hope to evolve new solutions and, in doing so, work to continuously improve society. Though this is our intent, many new ideas may be rejected or become failed solutions. But each of these failures and rejections brings the entire service ecosystem closer to a solution through a series of feedback loops. Humans do this work, not machines. Humans change their values and beliefs, learn, and orient toward different futures. Most important, it is when this happens that innovation comes to fruition. Hope, grit, and perseverance make innovation possible. When humans take risks, they open the service ecosystem to infinite possibilities. This improves plasticity in the service ecosystem so that it can take new forms

Kjellberg, H., and C.F. Helgesson. 2007. On the Nature of Markets and Their Practices. *Marketing Theory* 7 (2): 137–162.

Maglio, Paul P., and Jim Spohrer. 2008. Fundamentals of Service Science. *Journal of the Academy of Marketing Science* 36: 18–20.

Malthouse, Edward C., and Bobby J. Calder. 2011. Engagement and Experiences: Comment on Brodie, Hollenbeek, Juric, and Ilic. *Journal of Service Research* 14 (3): 277–279.

McColl-Kennedy, J.R., S.L. Vargo, T.S. Dagger, J.C. Sweeney, and Y. Van Kasteren. 2012. Health Care Customer Value Cocreation Practice Styles. *Journal of Service Research* 15 (4): 370–389.

Meynhardt, T., J.D. Chandler, and P. Strathoff. 2016. Systemic Principles of Value Co-creation: Synergetics of Value and Service Ecosystems. *Journal of Business Research* 69 (8): 2981–2989.

Nenonen, Suvi, Hans Kjellberg, Jacqueline Pels, Lilliemay Cheung, Sara Lindeman, Cristina Mele, Laszlo Sajtos, and Kaj Storbacka. 2014. A New Perspective on Market Dynamics: Market Plasticity and the Stability-Fluidity Dialectics. *Marketing Theory* 14 (3): 269–289.

Nilsson, E., and D. Ballantyne. 2014. Reexamining the Place of Servicescape in Marketing: A Service-Dominant Logic Perspective. *Journal of Services Marketing* 28 (5): 374–379.

Ortner, S.B. 1984. Theory in Anthropology Since the Sixties. *Comparative Studies in Society and History* 26 (1): 126–166.

Parasuraman, A., V.A. Zeithaml, and L.L. Berry. 1985. A Conceptual Model of Service Quality and Its Implications for Future Research. *The Journal of Marketing* 49: 41–50.

Pascarella, Ernest T., and Patrick T. Terenzini. 1991. *How College Affects Students: Findings and Insights from Twenty Years of Research*. San Francisco: Jossey-Bass.

Payne, Adrian, Kaj Storbacka, and Pennie Frow. 2008. Managing the Co-creation of Value. *Journal of the Academy of Marketing Science* 36 (1): 83–96.

Porter, M.E. 1985. *Competitive Advantage: Creating and Sustaining Superior Performance*. New York: FreePress.

Prahalad, C.K., and V. Ramaswamy. 2004. Co-creating Unique Value with Customers. *Strategy & Leadership* 32 (3): 4–9.

Rosenbaum, M.S., and C. Massiah. 2011. An Expanded Servicescape Perspective. *Journal of Service Management* 22 (4): 471–490.

Schatzki, T.R. 1996. *Social Practices: A Wittgensteinian Approach to Human Activity and the Social*. Cambridge: Cambridge University Press.

Schatzki, T.R., K. Knorr-Cetina, and E.V. Savigny. 2001. *The Practice Turn in Contemporary Theory*. East Sussex: Psychology Press.

Schau, H.P., A.M. Muñiz, and E.J. Arnould. 2009. How Brand Community Practices Create Value. *Journal of Marketing* 73 (5): 30–51.

Schaufeli, Wilmar B., and Arnold B. Bakker. 2004. Job Demands, Job Resources, and Their Relationship with Burnout and Engagement: A Multi-sample Study. *Journal of Organizational Behavior* 25 (3): 293–315.

Schaufeli, Wilmar B., Marisa Salanova, Vicente Gonzalez-Roma, and Arnold Bakker. 2002. The Measurement of Engagement and Burnout: A Two Sample Confirmatory Factor Analytic Approach. *Journal of Happiness Studies* 3 (1): 71–92.

Scott, Richard W. 2001. *Institutions and Organizations*. Thousand Oaks: Sage.

Smith, A. 1776. *An Inquiry into the Wealth of Nations*. London: Strahan and Cadell.

Surprenant, C.F., and M.R. Solomon. 1987. Predictability and Personalization in the Service Encounter. *The Journal of Marketing* 51: 86–96.

Tombs, A.G., and J.R. McColl-Kennedy. 2010. Social and Spatial Influence of Customers on Other Customers in the Social-Servicescape. *Australasian Marketing Journal (AMJ)* 18 (3): 120–131.

Vargo, S.L., and R.F. Lusch. 2004a. Evolving to a New Dominant Logic for Marketing. *Journal of Marketing* 68 (1): 1–17.

———. 2004b. The Four Service Marketing Myths: Remnants of a Goods-Based, Manufacturing Model. *Journal of Service Research* 6 (4): 324–335.

———. 2008. Service-Dominant Logic: Continuing the Evolution. *Journal of the Academy of Marketing Science* 36 (1): 1–10.

———. 2011. It's All B2B… and Beyond: Toward a Systems Perspective of the Market. *Industrial Marketing Management* 40 (2): 181–187.

———. 2016. Institutions and Axioms: An Extension and Update of Service-Dominant Logic. *Journal of the Academy of Marketing Science* 44 (1): 5–23.

———. 2017. Service-Dominant Logic 2025. *International Journal of Research in Marketing* 34 (1): 46–67.

Vargo, S.L., R.F. Lusch, and F.W. Morgan. 2006. Historical Perspectives on Service-Dominant Logic. In *The Service-Dominant Logic of Marketing: Dialog, Debate, and Directions*, 29–42. Armonk: ME Sharpe.

Vargo, S.L., P.P. Maglio, and M.A. Akaka. 2008. On Value and Value Co-creation: A Service Systems and Service Logic Perspective. *European Management Journal* 26 (3): 145–152.

Warde, A. 2005. Consumption and Theories of Practice. *Journal of Consumer Culture* 5 (2): 131–153.

CHAPTER 6

The Importance of Being Human

Humans imperfectly but incessantly are always trying to adc problems. It is part of our nature. We cannot escape that each o our own unique perspectives, faces challenges unique to our pas and future dispositions, as well as the contexts in which we are e We see the challenge or the problem, and then we attempt to r problem or address the challenge. But we do so in a myriad of reflects each of our own identities, dreams, aspirations, ar Sometimes we solve the problems. At other times, the problem and cannot be solved. Despite the latter, we are persistent abou forward. We simply will not back down. It is the human spiri humanity of hope that propel us into the future and that eng innovation. It is not that we are trying to purposefully pursue ir or creativity; it is that we have problems that we want to address

It is also noteworthy that humans ultimately support one anot it comes to new approaches being introduced to the market a ordinary humans seek extraordinary ways of doing simple thing willing to be engaged in the wishes and needs of others. We seek the good in every action. And most of all, we are determined forward. That determination and persistence enable us as a s embrace the multitude of actions, behaviors, and services that a hazardly in our everyday lives.

Since human beings are creatures of habit, our preferences fo and repetition establish processes in our daily lives that

J. D. Chandler, *Innovation, Social Networks, and Service Ecosystems*,
https://doi.org/10.1007/978-3-030-47797-4_6

and retain new forms. This is the most promising way for the service ecosystem to respond to continuous disruption.

Because of technology, humans have taken on some functions of the organization and now—despite technology—play a new enhanced role in today's twenty-first-century economy than they did in yesteryear. Unless we can become more spontaneous and random, organizations and government can use data to predict, inform, or even control our future behaviors. Humans had typically been aloof beneficiaries of benefits afforded to them by organizations (McColl-Kennedy et al. 2012). Toffler (1980) was among the first to recognize and discuss humans as prosumers in order to describe a new economic phenomenon in contemporary society. He articulates that humans were the first producers ever, and that humans in early cultures produced more for themselves and served their own needs. He further discusses how humans in contemporary society had somewhat become lazy recipients of passive value that were inserted into society by organizations. Humans had become passive consumers accepting what was being passed to them from organizations. At the same time, however, he proclaims there has been a renaissance of sorts by recognizing a contemporaneous rise in the number of humans who are returning back to the behaviors, habits, routines, and processes of the "good old days" and now glorify that they are making many of their own goods or serving themselves.

Some assert that this is how humans have begun to reclaim their identities from the organizations. They co-create value for themselves and others in many ways, including enrolling in self-help programs, developing micro ways of manufacturing special customized products, and creating new patterns of do-it-yourself services. This value co-creation also includes humans who modify or adapt organizational products and services to fit their own unique needs. Because these efforts generally do not fit the profit maximization patterns of firms, these market needs have largely been ignored. As a result, humans are actively addressing these issues in their own unique contexts across wider service ecosystems.

All too often, many pundits assume that innovation is synonymous with technology and the digital economy. They attribute the constant state of disruption that we are in to the pervasiveness of technology in society. Conversely, many equate the ubiquity of technology to continuous disruption. However, as a human society, we still face the same challenges that we have always encountered since the very beginning of time. These are not necessarily digital challenges. They are humanistic challenges like overcoming loneliness, finding love, and enjoying the comfort of a home. These challenges remain as simple as they were in yesteryear. In other words, we still face the same challenge that has always plagued humanity: how to create meaning in our lives. We, as human beings, are driven to innately and continuously survive; once we prove to ourselves that we can survive, we pursue meaning and happiness.

This social yearning highlights theoretical research that breaks down the human-firm dyad to reconceptualize how humans should be portrayed in light of service ecosystems. To put it another way, the notion that "firms produce" and "humans consume" is no longer logically or empirically valid. For example, Xie and associates (2008) found that the prosumption cycle involves value creation behaviors performed by the customer [that] result in the manufacture of products that can transform experiences. They describe the myriad of ways that humans can address issues and problems that are so distinctive and unique that most firms might incur too many costs to address these issues. This leaves a gap in the market that cannot be filled by the traditional market dyad of firm–customer relationships.

Ritzer (2014) claims in the same vein that humans have only become passive in recent socioeconomic history. Consequently, Ritzer describes prosumption as a continuum of events wherein pure output and pure consumption are not distinguishable. In yesteryear, in simpler economies that were not facilitated by indirect exchange and were not characterized by a sudden growth of a multisided platforms, humans were largely independent from the global service ecosystem. They may have been tightly connected within their own communities or contexts because they needed to be so. But at the same time, it was not necessary for them to be connected beyond their communities or contexts to the wider indistinguishable world out there. While prosumption has traditionally been studied as more than a single act, it actually and fundamentally consists of many different individual physical or mental actions or social activities that transpire during the course of exchange relationships. Moreover, because of coordination or cooperation with others, prosumption gives rise to unique sociopsychological experiences that strengthen ties within the community or context. Without technology, the ties within smaller communities may have been more dense and tightly woven. But with technology, the ties within contexts have become more dense and tightly woven. The base of service ecosystems, via presumption, is wider, stronger, and more dense.

In this way, prosumption can be viewed as a more nuanced, distinctive form of engagement (Pitt et al. 2006).

This occurs because humans who are engaged in their contexts are integral to service ecosystems. Humans are the activators, the catalysts, and the dreamers. They preside at the foundation of important industries such as healthcare, education, or energy, to name a few. These large-scale service ecosystems rely on humans who understand how such sectors impact quality of life. Humans sense the invisible threats that might ultimately emerge as problems and the obscured opportunities that might ultimately emerge as solutions. Engaged humans are aware that they need to adapt and are willing to work toward their goals.

In response to the continuous state of disruption brought about by the digital economy, organizations need to build their human capacity to respond quickly to new value propositions and innovation efforts. Organizations should always be looking for agile ways to work. Organizations should also encourage cross functionality on teams that are comprised of T-shaped professionals with deep knowledge bases and skill sets in different areas. This is difficult to achieve because organizations are typically built around functional areas, in which individuals possess and develop similar skill sets. Humans need to hone their specialties in becoming experts in their area, but also enhance their broad understanding of other areas in order to become T shaped professionals. This approach also makes it easier for the organization to develop competencies in a specific area and to hone the plasticity in their service ecosystems.

Humans and Plasticity

Since value significantly shapes the individual behaviors of actors in a system, value implicitly coordinates the individual behaviors of the various actors or devices—including humans—in a way that the actions of all are mutually beneficial to others embedded in the same service ecosystem. No matter which level of magnification, the properties, processes, and dynamics of the service ecosystem connect these various actors together. Humans, data, and machines differ from one another in many ways. But, because value is a systemic organizing principle, value is embedded in and cannot be separated from either the individual micro level or the collective macro level. In other words, value is so powerful that it can elicit a similar response from the various actors in a service ecosystem.

Plasticity emerges from the degree to which systemic actors and elements can be harmonized, as well as the likelihood of maintaining this harmonization. Every service ecosystem has a particular plasticity that influences how its various systemic actors and elements respond to value. Noting that each individual actor and systemic element is unique, the combination of individual actors and systemic elements is also unique—which gives rise to unique service ecosystems. The nature and character of the service ecosystem is a factor of the set of individual actors and systemic elements that comprise the service ecosystem. For this reason, each individual service ecosystem has a different "potentiality for being remolded and responding in a different way thereafter". Since there are various feedback loops, it is difficult to predict how systemic elements together will move through time and react to change. As a result, it is not easy to predict how value propositions might be evaluated and how innovation might occur across different service ecosystems. What may work in one service ecosystem may not work in another service ecosystem.

For these reasons, humans should be more observant of the dimensions on which service ecosystems can differ from one another. Fluidity is the capacity of the service ecosystem to take on a different form or to be molded, and stability is the capacity of the service ecosystem to retain a particular form or to remain at a particular equilibrium. At their very nature, humans often give service ecosystems fluidity and stability. This is because humans sense problems, challenges, and opportunities, and then try to address or solve them. They transform service ecosystems when they attempt to solve problems and provide solutions. Fluidity and stability are interdependent dimensions of plasticity. They are not opposites. A service ecosystem can be high in both fluidity and stability, or low in both fluidity and stability. Also, a service ecosystem can be high on one dimension while being low in the other. Fluidity and stability together represent how service ecosystems respond to humans trying to solve problems, or, in other words, value creation efforts.

If systemic elements all respond positively to a value proposition, there is wider systemic change and harmonization of innovation efforts. In a high-technology environment, consider that the value proposition could be a new software or a new data point. If this new software or data point generates positive reactions from other systemic elements, the system is more easily adaptable to the new software or data. If systemic elements all respond negatively to a value proposition, there is very little or no systemic change and innovation efforts are largely rejected. Continuing the previous example, if systemic elements respond negatively to a new software for new data, then the system will not change and innovation efforts are generally impeded. If the reaction of elements is mixed (some negative, some positive), there is some degree of systemic change. In high-technology environments, this is usually the case. Because the reactions of systemic elements to new software or new data are often mixed, customer service and technological support services can help to ameliorate the various responses. In this way, technical support staff have begun to play a role that is closely aligned with helping individuals in the system adapt to change. For example, in many mobile device applications, chat-bots serving as customer service support may collect data about different user interfaces or user environment challenges that are not yet accommodated by the mobile application. In real time, these bots make programmers and developers aware of the flaws in the mobile application so that the software can be adapted to the user environment challenges, or value proposition. This encompasses a continuous revision of the software. In this way, the service ecosystem is always thriving, balancing change with some fluidity and some stability.

However, these incessant invitations that arrive in the forms of value propositions and the continuous introductions of innovation efforts do not necessarily occur as high magnitude events. Rather, the invitations might be narrow or small, and innovation may take the form of an individual actor simply voicing an opinion. Over time, these smaller behaviors may erode existing parameters that give order to an ecosystem. In this way, innovation is ongoing in a continuous process by which both small and large perturbations may influence the service ecosystem. Because systemic elements may interact differently, a different logic or order parameter may emerge as some form of innovation. As mentioned previously, innovation is a complex process that includes both failures and successes. There are many different states of equilibrium, fluidity, and stability for a particular service ecosystem. Over time, a service ecosystem may reach different degrees of each. Accordingly, these influence plasticity, which in turn influences the system's ability to evolve in response to a new value proposition or innovation effort.

In innovation research, the traditional investigation often explores the impact or incredibility of the innovation. However, the proposed perspective emphasizes plasticity, which centers on the systemic reception or response to innovation. Stated differently, plasticity is important because it represents the fertility of the soil that receives a seed of innovation. The number of invitations, or value propositions, helps to prepare the soil, or the service ecosystem, for the innovation. Although some of these may seem like failed value propositions, the effort may have prepared the system for innovation. Without the previous efforts, it is possible that the successful value proposition would not have thrived. In other words, the previous interactions may have improved the plasticity of the service ecosystem. On the other hand, if a service ecosystem is low in plasticity, then an innovation cannot flourish.

By understanding plasticity, it is possible to begin thinking holistically about the dimensions and traits of service ecosystems that can contribute to innovation and value creation. It is also important to note that service ecosystems exist on a temporal continuum and, as such, can have more plasticity at one point time and less plasticity at another point in time. Thus, plasticity is not a static variable. It can influence innovation in different ways, depending on the point in time at which the innovation and service ecosystem interact. Generally speaking, innovation is influenced by plasticity in four ways: recursivity, temporality, complementarity, and continuity. Each of these is described below.

Recursivity

Recursivity refers to the reaction of systemic elements to dissonance in the service ecosystem. This can include beliefs, emotions, cognitions, behaviors, and actions regarding potential value creation. When a value proposition is introduced to a service ecosystem, it is rare for all systemic elements to react uniformly. Some may react negatively while others may react positively. Moreover, a systemic element may react to a value proposition as a threat or an opportunity. As a result, some systemic elements may either strengthen or weaken their reactions in order to remain harmonized with other systemic elements. At this point, the value proposition is merely a perturbation or disturbance to the service ecosystem. It has not yet become established as an order parameter, and the system is attempting to self-adjust in response to it. The overall effect that it might have on the service ecosystem is not yet clear. Individual systemic elements adjust to provide greater fluidity and stability to the service ecosystem in a recursive way. This adjustment comprises a feedback loop that facilitates plasticity; the fluidity allows the service ecosystem to move toward taking on a new form while the stability maintains synchronicity in the service ecosystem. It is not yet clear, at a systemic level, how the value proposition will be received.

Each systemic element reacts locally to the value proposition; in other words, each systemic element typically reacts in a way that optimizes its local position and situation. For instance, some systemic elements may interact with other elements in order to harmonize their response to the value proposition. This feedback loop can create a new path and introduce more stability to the service ecosystem. At the same time, to enhance service ecosystem fluidity, other systemic elements may disassociate with one another. In this feedback loop, a different order may emerge that elicits response from other systemic elements. Multiple disparate feedback loops in a service ecosystem disseminate throughout the system and catalyze clusters of change. Meanwhile, there is convergence around value propositions as they are introduced to the service ecosystem. Fluidity of the service ecosystem increases, and there is possible disruption of prevailing order parameters. In other words, the innovation process gains momentum.

The feedback loops that transpire during innovation are thus important for subsequent value propositions that are later introduced to the service ecosystem and are pivotal for moving the innovation process forward. Transformed beliefs or learned knowledge often emerge in response to value propositions, and these ultimately stimulate feedback loops. When habits, culture, or attitudes change in response to feedback loops, ideas and institutions also change during the innovation process. When systemic elements intermingle, they may influence one another and change the nature of the service ecosystem. The plasticity of a service ecosystem influences recursivity, or the number and magnitude of feedback loops.

Temporality

When a value proposition is introduced to a service ecosystem, it can also catalyze stability, or retain form. This is especially true for service ecosystems that are highly fluid and like to take new forms. A service ecosystem's plasticity influences the speed of systemic response once a value proposition has been introduced to a service ecosystem. In this way, plasticity influences a value proposition by the velocity of the response by systemic elements. When a value proposition is introduced to a service ecosystem, it may not always be well received. In most stable service ecosystems, existing patterns among systemic elements resonate with other existing patterns and together these are remembered throughout the service ecosystem. However, in service ecosystems that are less stable, the recursivity and feedback loops that occur in response to a value proposition may establish different values and behaviors that then reverberate through the service ecosystem. As innovation is pursued over time, the service ecosystem can change in nature. This can occur at either the micro, meso, or macro levels of the service ecosystem. When systemic elements at each of these levels become harmonized, the service ecosystem becomes more stable over time.

Complementarity

At first, a value proposition is introduced. Then some systemic elements initially react to the value proposition. Ultimately, the other systemic elements that were interconnected with the initial elements then also react to the value proposition and their changed relationship with other systemic elements. This increases the capacity of the service ecosystem to retain a new form by establishing different norms, rules, and beliefs in the service ecosystem. As a result, the service ecosystem is more stable than it was previously. Increasingly, there are shorter feedback loops that then increase alignment throughout the service ecosystem including synchronizing values, beliefs, and behaviors at the micro, meso, and macro levels. Although this synchronization is not explicit, the recursive feedback loops increase complementarity among systemic elements. Sometimes, the complementarity is fruitful and the innovation efforts are successful. At other times, the complementarity does not work and the innovation efforts fail since the systemic elements are not harmonized in their response to the value proposition. Plasticity of a service ecosystem influences the complementarity that can then influence the value proposition. A high degree of fluidity is needed to achieve complementarity so that individual systemic elements can more easily harmonize with the other elements.

Continuity

Although a value proposition has been introduced to the service ecosystem, it is possible that some systemic elements may not be calibrated adequately with others. This creates upheaval in the service ecosystem, which deteriorates into further disarray. Attempting to achieve a new or revised equilibrium, feedback loops catalyze different responses, perturbations, and processes. It is not immediately clear which of these will eventually

Most researchers focus on what humans buy, rather than what humans do. But, as output and consumption are seen as interdependent service-connected systems, both the firm and the customer are seen as providing feedback into the systems of one another (Grönroos and Voima 2013). Humans are innovative individuals who create and develop their own service experiences. Specifically, on the one hand, they recreate the feeling of social capital and appear to emphasize past social moments. On the other hand, they seek connectedness and community which drives their engagement in service ecosystems (Deci and Ryan 2000; Muniz and O'Guinn 2001). Humans who act as innovators engage in value co-creation vis-à-vis service interactions that help them to create specific and personalized products that address their unique problems.

According to Ritzer (2014), the literary emphasis on pure production and pure consumption has overshadowed prosumption. Human beings, however, have only consumed what they produce and produced what they consume. Indeed, a crucial difference between humans and other species is the human capacity to absorb and create artifacts of their own making. It is thus important to understand human actions, procedures, and motives because they shape marketplace and society. Humans seek value when they create beautiful things from ordinary household items. Generally, service encounters were defined as transformative and exceptional encounters, usually characterized by high emotional intensity (Arnould and Price 1993). But typically these service encounters are extraordinary as defined by the firm. Generally, many service experiences are quite ordinary, common, and casual. This is especially so when they are incorporated into everyday routines. Oftentimes, humans regularly participate in service ecosystems that depend on adapting firms' proprietary offerings into customized artifacts. Since their innovative efforts are strengthened by individuals who can draw on Internet access, these humans have become important to study as service ecosystems have come to occupy the forefront of society.

These service experiences depend heavily on humans. Many businesses effectively invite humans to participate in their service ecosystems by offering toolkits (Franke and Piller 2004). From a traditional manufacturing perspective, toolkits make it easier for humans to participate in a service ecosystem by dividing a project into subtasks. Humans can then take any combination of and use them to create unique products that are pleasing (Campbell 2005). These toolkits transfer the service experience from the company's confined service environment to the human's personal universe

dominate. It is also possible that extant processes may be refined in some way. As these various new value propositions emanate out from their points of origin, the service ecosystem is filled with many, many value propositions. They may catalyze innovation processes in different places in a recursive process that may continue until a successful outcome is achieved.

Thus, innovation is constant, and the plasticity of a service ecosystem influences how the fluidity and stability of a service ecosystem ebbs and flows in response to a continuous wave of value propositions. Innovation is a systemic process that never ends, never fails, and never truly succeeds—especially since a service ecosystem is always in flux. Innovation is the constant state of disruption that we have come to know in the digital economy. Innovation does not require a complete ending of the story, nor does it require full alignment of a service ecosystem. Ultimately, the continuity and the disruption of the digital economy are unlikely to fade so it is more helpful to harness their power than to wish them away.

When a value proposition is proposed in a service ecosystem, it often evolves in response to the many pressures of the service ecosystem. Since service ecosystems cannot be controlled by a single actor, innovation also cannot be controlled by a single actor. So, as a result, the value proposition that emerges as an innovation can sometimes look different, much like a unique and new idea that has been revised, revised, and revised again by elements in the service ecosystem as it gained wider acceptance. Generally speaking, when existing solutions are insufficient for solving existing problems, service ecosystems begin to stop being self-organized. Departing from old order parameters, systemic elements begin to vibrate differently and new ways of activity begin to emerge. Sometimes, there are inconsistencies when each level of the service ecosystem is viewed separately; for example, the micro-level individual behaviors may not coincide or harmonize with macro-level cultural values. These inconsistencies can begin to stimulate a change in systemic logic. Because the inconsistencies affect some elements more than others, only some systemic elements will react.

Understanding innovation from this perspective clarifies that there are many starts and stops in the process, and that the process is complex and multifaceted. Innovation is not a stage-gate linear process, nor is it a messy design-thinking exercise in creativity. Rather, innovation is a series of trials and errors, failures, and successes. These, together, prepare the service ecosystem for a new successful outcome for problems that are rather old. Innovation is the response to pressure, and the process by which we come to terms with our endeavors to find meaning and happiness. Like a circular change, the innovation pendulum swings back and forth balancing out the different forms and states of a service ecosystem. By showing innovation as an ongoing process, the networked and systemic nature of innovation is highlighted. When innovation is viewed in this way, the role of the service ecosystem becomes clear: the service ecosystem is where a value proposition initiates how an innovation ultimately takes form and function. Viewing innovation as isolated from the service ecosystem does not fully capture how systemic elements might resist, adapt, or react to value propositions. Further, viewing innovation as isolated from the service ecosystem does not show the necessity of failures and feedback loops on the road to beneficial outcomes. Finally, and most important, viewing innovation as isolated from the service ecosystem does not demonstrate the implicit and explicit coordination and collaboration required to emerge potentially beneficial outcomes. Viewing innovation in isolation from the true innovation process is like looking at an incomplete picture without a background.

To address the constant state of disruption that characterizes today's digital economy, humans still need to depend on another in order to achieve and continuously develop the cross-functionality needed by the organization to deploy teams. This is necessary because it is difficult to move large projects from one large functional area of the organization to another large functional area. Because of high coordination costs and complex siloed working environments, project managers find it difficult to cross these organizational boundaries. It is difficult for project managers to communicate in the "different languages" needed for each functional area. Humans are needed to aid knowledge transfer when projects move from one functional area of the organization to another. To assure that knowledge is maintained and that decisions are communicated clearly, it is important to encourage individuals to nurture trust in the organization. They work to break down silos housed within functional areas and try to see projects in their larger contexts. Humans need to look beyond their immediate tasks, and proactively seek help when completing their own tasks. They should embrace problem-solving to enhance their responsibilities on the project.

One way to overcome this challenge is to cultivate teams that are T shaped. In T-shaped teams, each team member has a different set of expertise, knowledge, and skills. As the individuals work together on teams, they acquire different knowledge bases and skill sets. The team overall

becomes more versatile and capable of solving many problems The team has a learning-by-doing attitude, since they together many problems and create solutions that did not exist before. Thi coordination challenges since the dependencies between functic changes in nature. Because there is actually one individual per f area on a team, it is easier for individuals to relay information team to the rest of the functional area. This approach also reduc of knowledge between functional areas and contribute to a decis ing service that is more streamlined and transparent. As a resul less blame and more pro-active behavior. Over time, as more individuals collaborate with one another, their own skill sets a edge bases are broadened. The best possible outcome is that the als take ownership of the project because they had been involve project from start to finish.

It is important to either hire individuals who can work on teams or train individuals to work on T-shaped teams. Of course erable to hire T-shaped professionals from the onset but this since many individuals receive traditional training and degrees. it is difficult to detect empathy from reviewing one's resume, it detect empathy when meeting the individual whether this occu through the interview service or informally when casually mee one. Empathy can be seen when the individual talks positively a people with whom they have collaborated. If an individual f talks only on their own accomplishments, then it is a red flag. I an individual talks positively about team experiences or how helped them to accomplish their own goals, then it is a sign Relatedly, for individuals are already at the company, one wa empathy is to pay attention to the individuals who are al recruited to various teams. It is a sign that their peers apprecia laborative nature and that their knowledge and skill sets are also important to pay attention to how people participate in t tion and in the wider service ecosystem. Are they contributin places? Are they good members of the community? Are they s knowledge and giving advice? It is also a good idea to develop a review, which can evaluate how well the individual has mai updated their deep knowledge base and skill set. A 360-degre also assess whether they have developed collaboration and cor skills, as well as other skills related to working on teams.

CHAPTER 6

The Importance of Being Human

Humans imperfectly but incessantly are always trying to address their problems. It is part of our nature. We cannot escape that each of us, from our own unique perspectives, faces challenges unique to our past, present, and future dispositions, as well as the contexts in which we are embedded. We see the challenge or the problem, and then we attempt to resolve the problem or address the challenge. But we do so in a myriad of ways that reflects each of our own identities, dreams, aspirations, and needs. Sometimes we solve the problems. At other times, the problems elude us and cannot be solved. Despite the latter, we are persistent about moving forward. We simply will not back down. It is the human spirit and the humanity of hope that propel us into the future and that engage us in innovation. It is not that we are trying to purposefully pursue innovation or creativity; it is that we have problems that we want to address.

It is also noteworthy that humans ultimately support one another when it comes to new approaches being introduced to the market and when ordinary humans seek extraordinary ways of doing simple things. We are willing to be engaged in the wishes and needs of others. We seek to believe the good in every action. And most of all, we are determined to move forward. That determination and persistence enable us as a society to embrace the multitude of actions, behaviors, and services that arise haphazardly in our everyday lives.

Since human beings are creatures of habit, our preferences for routine and repetition establish processes in our daily lives that make us

J. D. Chandler, *Innovation, Social Networks, and Service Ecosystems*,
https://doi.org/10.1007/978-3-030-47797-4_6

comfortable and reify our existence. We crave these processes for they give us stability. They strengthen our service ecosystems because our interactions invigorate them. As a result, these processes are difficult to alter because they are hallmarks of our own personal comforts. We created them, we left them there, and we are happy to continue engraving them into the narrative of the human race. These routine behaviors give us comfort and help us to find value and meaning in our everyday lives. They are the basis of service ecosystems and help service ecosystems to retain their form. In the United States and many other Westernized countries, we relish the certainty embedded in these routines and habits. For many human beings, their physical and mental well-being depends on the existence of routine. Because of this, it is certainly possible that the organizations with whom we engage collect, house, and harness data about us and our most personal daily behaviors. To a large extent, many of us enjoy how these data help our favorite organizations like Google or Apple make our lives easier; this occurs when smart devices automatically turn on lights in our houses or when our smart phones give us turn-by-turn directions as we drive to work. All the while, organizations are collecting data about our everyday lives. Many Americans and citizens of other countries are happy to share their data with companies in order to reap the value of autonomous integrations that help us to lead harmonized, simpler lives. The value, again, stems from the predictability of our behaviors, routines, and processes.

When we as individuals reach out to those in our immediate contexts to consider our ideas and value propositions, we engage others in our own attempts to remedy the issues that we have identified in our context. Others may not perceive those situations as issues, and, at times, we may work inadvertently against one another in trying to solve a problem. In the end, we each hope to evolve new solutions and, in doing so, work to continuously improve society. Though this is our intent, many new ideas may be rejected or become failed solutions. But each of these failures and rejections brings the entire service ecosystem closer to a solution through a series of feedback loops. Humans do this work, not machines. Humans change their values and beliefs, learn, and orient toward different futures. Most important, it is when this happens that innovation comes to fruition. Hope, grit, and perseverance make innovation possible. When humans take risks, they open the service ecosystem to infinite possibilities. This improves plasticity in the service ecosystem so that it can take new forms

Kjellberg, H., and C.F. Helgesson. 2007. On the Nature of Markets and Their Practices. *Marketing Theory* 7 (2): 137–162.

Maglio, Paul P., and Jim Spohrer. 2008. Fundamentals of Service Science. *Journal of the Academy of Marketing Science* 36: 18–20.

Malthouse, Edward C., and Bobby J. Calder. 2011. Engagement and Experiences: Comment on Brodie, Hollenbeek, Juric, and Ilic. *Journal of Service Research* 14 (3): 277–279.

McColl-Kennedy, J.R., S.L. Vargo, T.S. Dagger, J.C. Sweeney, and Y. Van Kasteren. 2012. Health Care Customer Value Cocreation Practice Styles. *Journal of Service Research* 15 (4): 370–389.

Meynhardt, T., J.D. Chandler, and P. Strathoff. 2016. Systemic Principles of Value Co-creation: Synergetics of Value and Service Ecosystems. *Journal of Business Research* 69 (8): 2981–2989.

Nenonen, Suvi, Hans Kjellberg, Jacqueline Pels, Lilliemay Cheung, Sara Lindeman, Cristina Mele, Laszlo Sajtos, and Kaj Storbacka. 2014. A New Perspective on Market Dynamics: Market Plasticity and the Stability-Fluidity Dialectics. *Marketing Theory* 14 (3): 269–289.

Nilsson, E., and D. Ballantyne. 2014. Reexamining the Place of Servicescape in Marketing: A Service-Dominant Logic Perspective. *Journal of Services Marketing* 28 (5): 374–379.

Ortner, S.B. 1984. Theory in Anthropology Since the Sixties. *Comparative Studies in Society and History* 26 (1): 126–166.

Parasuraman, A., V.A. Zeithaml, and L.L. Berry. 1985. A Conceptual Model of Service Quality and Its Implications for Future Research. *The Journal of Marketing* 49: 41–50.

Pascarella, Ernest T., and Patrick T. Terenzini. 1991. *How College Affects Students: Findings and Insights from Twenty Years of Research*. San Francisco: Jossey-Bass.

Payne, Adrian, Kaj Storbacka, and Pennie Frow. 2008. Managing the Co-creation of Value. *Journal of the Academy of Marketing Science* 36 (1): 83–96.

Porter, M.E. 1985. *Competitive Advantage: Creating and Sustaining Superior Performance*. New York: FreePress.

Prahalad, C.K., and V. Ramaswamy. 2004. Co-creating Unique Value with Customers. *Strategy & Leadership* 32 (3): 4–9.

Rosenbaum, M.S., and C. Massiah. 2011. An Expanded Servicescape Perspective. *Journal of Service Management* 22 (4): 471–490.

Schatzki, T.R. 1996. *Social Practices: A Wittgensteinian Approach to Human Activity and the Social*. Cambridge: Cambridge University Press.

Schatzki, T.R., K. Knorr-Cetina, and E.V. Savigny. 2001. *The Practice Turn in Contemporary Theory*. East Sussex: Psychology Press.

Schau, H.P., A.M. Muñiz, and E.J. Arnould. 2009. How Brand Community Practices Create Value. *Journal of Marketing* 73 (5): 30–51.

Schaufeli, Wilmar B., and Arnold B. Bakker. 2004. Job Demands, Job Resources, and Their Relationship with Burnout and Engagement: A Multi-sample Study. *Journal of Organizational Behavior* 25 (3): 293–315.

Schaufeli, Wilmar B., Marisa Salanova, Vicente Gonzalez-Roma, and Arnold Bakker. 2002. The Measurement of Engagement and Burnout: A Two Sample Confirmatory Factor Analytic Approach. *Journal of Happiness Studies* 3 (1): 71–92.

Scott, Richard W. 2001. *Institutions and Organizations*. Thousand Oaks: Sage.

Smith, A. 1776. *An Inquiry into the Wealth of Nations*. London: Strahan and Cadell.

Surprenant, C.F., and M.R. Solomon. 1987. Predictability and Personalization in the Service Encounter. *The Journal of Marketing* 51: 86–96.

Tombs, A.G., and J.R. McColl-Kennedy. 2010. Social and Spatial Influence of Customers on Other Customers in the Social-Servicescape. *Australasian Marketing Journal (AMJ)* 18 (3): 120–131.

Vargo, S.L., and R.F. Lusch. 2004a. Evolving to a New Dominant Logic for Marketing. *Journal of Marketing* 68 (1): 1–17.

———. 2004b. The Four Service Marketing Myths: Remnants of a Goods-Based, Manufacturing Model. *Journal of Service Research* 6 (4): 324–335.

———. 2008. Service-Dominant Logic: Continuing the Evolution. *Journal of the Academy of Marketing Science* 36 (1): 1–10.

———. 2011. It's All B2B… and Beyond: Toward a Systems Perspective of the Market. *Industrial Marketing Management* 40 (2): 181–187.

———. 2016. Institutions and Axioms: An Extension and Update of Service-Dominant Logic. *Journal of the Academy of Marketing Science* 44 (1): 5–23.

———. 2017. Service-Dominant Logic 2025. *International Journal of Research in Marketing* 34 (1): 46–67.

Vargo, S.L., R.F. Lusch, and F.W. Morgan. 2006. Historical Perspectives on Service-Dominant Logic. In *The Service-Dominant Logic of Marketing: Dialog, Debate, and Directions*, 29–42. Armonk: ME Sharpe.

Vargo, S.L., P.P. Maglio, and M.A. Akaka. 2008. On Value and Value Co-creation: A Service Systems and Service Logic Perspective. *European Management Journal* 26 (3): 145–152.

Warde, A. 2005. Consumption and Theories of Practice. *Journal of Consumer Culture* 5 (2): 131–153.

becomes more versatile and capable of solving many problems quickly. The team has a learning-by-doing attitude, since they together can solve many problems and create solutions that did not exist before. This reduces coordination challenges since the dependencies between functional areas changes in nature. Because there is actually one individual per functional area on a team, it is easier for individuals to relay information from the team to the rest of the functional area. This approach also reduces the loss of knowledge between functional areas and contribute to a decision-making service that is more streamlined and transparent. As a result, there is less blame and more pro-active behavior. Over time, as more and more individuals collaborate with one another, their own skill sets and knowledge bases are broadened. The best possible outcome is that the individuals take ownership of the project because they had been involved with the project from start to finish.

It is important to either hire individuals who can work on T-shaped teams or train individuals to work on T-shaped teams. Of course, it is preferable to hire T-shaped professionals from the onset but this is difficult since many individuals receive traditional training and degrees. Although it is difficult to detect empathy from reviewing one's resume, it is easier to detect empathy when meeting the individual whether this occurs formally through the interview service or informally when casually meeting someone. Empathy can be seen when the individual talks positively about other people with whom they have collaborated. If an individual focuses and talks only on their own accomplishments, then it is a red flag. However, if an individual talks positively about team experiences or how others have helped them to accomplish their own goals, then it is a sign of empathy. Relatedly, for individuals are already at the company, one way to detect empathy is to pay attention to the individuals who are always being recruited to various teams. It is a sign that their peers appreciate their collaborative nature and that their knowledge and skill sets are sound. It is also important to pay attention to how people participate in the organization and in the wider service ecosystem. Are they contributing in various places? Are they good members of the community? Are they sharing their knowledge and giving advice? It is also a good idea to develop a 360-degree review, which can evaluate how well the individual has maintained and updated their deep knowledge base and skill set. A 360-degree review can also assess whether they have developed collaboration and communication skills, as well as other skills related to working on teams.

Most researchers focus on what humans buy, rather than what humans do. But, as output and consumption are seen as interdependent service-connected systems, both the firm and the customer are seen as providing feedback into the systems of one another (Grönroos and Voima 2013). Humans are innovative individuals who create and develop their own service experiences. Specifically, on the one hand, they recreate the feeling of social capital and appear to emphasize past social moments. On the other hand, they seek connectedness and community which drives their engagement in service ecosystems (Deci and Ryan 2000; Muniz and O'Guinn 2001). Humans who act as innovators engage in value co-creation vis-à-vis service interactions that help them to create specific and personalized products that address their unique problems.

According to Ritzer (2014), the literary emphasis on pure production and pure consumption has overshadowed prosumption. Human beings, however, have only consumed what they produce and produced what they consume. Indeed, a crucial difference between humans and other species is the human capacity to absorb and create artifacts of their own making. It is thus important to understand human actions, procedures, and motives because they shape marketplace and society. Humans seek value when they create beautiful things from ordinary household items. Generally, service encounters were defined as transformative and exceptional encounters, usually characterized by high emotional intensity (Arnould and Price 1993). But typically these service encounters are extraordinary as defined by the firm. Generally, many service experiences are quite ordinary, common, and casual. This is especially so when they are incorporated into everyday routines. Oftentimes, humans regularly participate in service ecosystems that depend on adapting firms' proprietary offerings into customized artifacts. Since their innovative efforts are strengthened by individuals who can draw on Internet access, these humans have become important to study as service ecosystems have come to occupy the forefront of society.

These service experiences depend heavily on humans. Many businesses effectively invite humans to participate in their service ecosystems by offering toolkits (Franke and Piller 2004). From a traditional manufacturing perspective, toolkits make it easier for humans to participate in a service ecosystem by dividing a project into subtasks. Humans can then take any combination of and use them to create unique products that are pleasing (Campbell 2005). These toolkits transfer the service experience from the company's confined service environment to the human's personal universe to terms with our endeavors to find meaning and happiness. Like a circular change, the innovation pendulum swings back and forth balancing out the different forms and states of a service ecosystem. By showing innovation as an ongoing process, the networked and systemic nature of innovation is highlighted. When innovation is viewed in this way, the role of the service ecosystem becomes clear: the service ecosystem is where a value proposition initiates how an innovation ultimately takes form and function. Viewing innovation as isolated from the service ecosystem does not fully capture how systemic elements might resist, adapt, or react to value propositions. Further, viewing innovation as isolated from the service ecosystem does not show the necessity of failures and feedback loops on the road to beneficial outcomes. Finally, and most important, viewing innovation as isolated from the service ecosystem does not demonstrate the implicit and explicit coordination and collaboration required to emerge potentially beneficial outcomes. Viewing innovation in isolation from the true innovation process is like looking at an incomplete picture without a background.

To address the constant state of disruption that characterizes today's digital economy, humans still need to depend on another in order to achieve and continuously develop the cross-functionality needed by the organization to deploy teams. This is necessary because it is difficult to move large projects from one large functional area of the organization to another large functional area. Because of high coordination costs and complex siloed working environments, project managers find it difficult to cross these organizational boundaries. It is difficult for project managers to communicate in the "different languages" needed for each functional area. Humans are needed to aid knowledge transfer when projects move from one functional area of the organization to another. To assure that knowledge is maintained and that decisions are communicated clearly, it is important to encourage individuals to nurture trust in the organization. They work to break down silos housed within functional areas and try to see projects in their larger contexts. Humans need to look beyond their immediate tasks, and proactively seek help when completing their own tasks. They should embrace problem-solving to enhance their responsibilities on the project.

One way to overcome this challenge is to cultivate teams that are T shaped. In T-shaped teams, each team member has a different set of expertise, knowledge, and skills. As the individuals work together on teams, they acquire different knowledge bases and skill sets. The team overall dominate. It is also possible that extant processes may be refined in some way. As these various new value propositions emanate out from their points of origin, the service ecosystem is filled with many, many value propositions. They may catalyze innovation processes in different places in a recursive process that may continue until a successful outcome is achieved.

Thus, innovation is constant, and the plasticity of a service ecosystem influences how the fluidity and stability of a service ecosystem ebbs and flows in response to a continuous wave of value propositions. Innovation is a systemic process that never ends, never fails, and never truly succeeds—especially since a service ecosystem is always in flux. Innovation is the constant state of disruption that we have come to know in the digital economy. Innovation does not require a complete ending of the story, nor does it require full alignment of a service ecosystem. Ultimately, the continuity and the disruption of the digital economy are unlikely to fade so it is more helpful to harness their power than to wish them away.

When a value proposition is proposed in a service ecosystem, it often evolves in response to the many pressures of the service ecosystem. Since service ecosystems cannot be controlled by a single actor, innovation also cannot be controlled by a single actor. So, as a result, the value proposition that emerges as an innovation can sometimes look different, much like a unique and new idea that has been revised, revised, and revised again by elements in the service ecosystem as it gained wider acceptance. Generally speaking, when existing solutions are insufficient for solving existing problems, service ecosystems begin to stop being self-organized. Departing from old order parameters, systemic elements begin to vibrate differently and new ways of activity begin to emerge. Sometimes, there are inconsistencies when each level of the service ecosystem is viewed separately; for example, the micro-level individual behaviors may not coincide or harmonize with macro-level cultural values. These inconsistencies can begin to stimulate a change in systemic logic. Because the inconsistencies affect some elements more than others, only some systemic elements will react.

Understanding innovation from this perspective clarifies that there are many starts and stops in the process, and that the process is complex and multifaceted. Innovation is not a stage-gate linear process, nor is it a messy design-thinking exercise in creativity. Rather, innovation is a series of trials and errors, failures, and successes. These, together, prepare the service ecosystem for a new successful outcome for problems that are rather old. Innovation is the response to pressure, and the process by which we come

(Bitner 1992). This allows humans to co-create or receive special, personalized products which extend the product's initial configuration (Franke et al. 2008).

Nevertheless, it is important to remember that humans frequently judge and engage in co-creation in ways that businesses do not anticipate. Consequently, customers behaving as suppliers are not simply receivers or co-producers, as in the logical context, but co-producers with their network knowledge (Schembri 2006). Whereas production exists on the market for economic trade, prosumption exists when production existed on the market. To this end, Edvardsson, Enquist, and Johnston (2005) illustrate how products or items can be embedded into service ecosystems from different locations on the market, be it from a manufacturer or the living room of a human who acts as producer (Etgar 2008). Humans engage in and customize their own service experiences when they incorporate their own personal objects into their service experiences.

Individual motivations to participate in service ecosystems relate to the intrinsic effects of cognitive growth as well as integrity and well-being (Deci and Ryan 2000). When evaluating value propositions and new ideas, they consider the existing order parameters in their service ecosystems. Humans use these service ecosystems to achieve autonomy and affirmation of their abilities. Autonomy requires independence from instruction and the ability to complete a project at will (Dahl and Moreau 2007). By completing within such service ecosystems, humans fulfill Maslowian needs such as self-actualization. Researchers also show positive associations between artistic and self-esteem behaviors (Bournelli et al. 2009; Kemple et al. 1996; Lau et al. 2004). Such studies indicate that the ingenuity and flexibility that can be gained from involvement in service ecosystems motivates humans. Humans are often driven by the psychological gratification arising from successful project completion (Dahl and Moreau 2007). Humans also indulge in service encounters to achieve sensations of satisfaction and pleasure. By mastering the technological skills associated with some service experiences, humans may attain competency feelings (Rostan 2010). Accordingly, these influence plasticity, which in turn influences the system's ability to evolve in response to a new value proposition or innovation effort.

A service experience may enhance learning as humans search for and develop skills needed to participate in particular service ecosystems (Dahl and Moreau 2007). Additionally, humans have been shown to appreciate competence in artistic actions commensurate with their skill levels (Watson and Shove 2008). In addition, research has shown that projects of self-identity can inspire engagement in innovative actions that may be inherent in some service experiences (Belk 1990). Ultimately, dealing with cycles of tension, illness, and life change (Nicol and Long 1996; Zausner 1998) will inspire the involvement of humans in innovative service ecosystems (Reynolds 2004; Reynolds et al. 2008). Sometimes, the reaction of systemic elements to dissonance in the service ecosystem can stimulate a need for more cognitive reassurance. This can include beliefs, emotions, cognitions, behaviors, or actions. When a value proposition is introduced to a service ecosystem, it is rare for all systemic elements to react uniformly. Some may react negatively, while others may react positively.

Humans are often socially motivated; that is, they pursue results that are extrinsic such as improving their social networks, making friends, and creating community (Arnould and Thompson 2005). Each systemic element reacts locally to a value proposition; in other words, each systemic element typically reacts in a way that optimizes its local position and situation. For instance, some systemic elements may interact with other elements in order to harmonize their response to the value proposition. This feedback loop can create a new path and introduce more stability to the service ecosystem. Prügl and Schreier (2006) consider that solutions produced by humans will develop high demand from other humans, a social dimension that has been ignored in the literature on services. Ultimately, some humans are inspired by a collective sense of accomplishment, or by the desire for others to recognize one's accomplishments (Dahl and Moreau 2007). Humans are also looking for a community and a mode for communication, social ties. and family networking. Humans also seek experiences of coexistence and engagement (Gainer 1995). It is also valid for humans to seek social bonding and feelings of solidarity. Relationship—or the urge to feel connected to others—often motivates humans; though service scholars have only recently begun to discuss service ecosystems that establish long-term relationships (Garzaniti et al. 2011; Muniz and O'Guinn 2001).

Corporate norms have evolved. The popular Etsy site equates organizations (as recipients) and individuals (as suppliers) as they both purchase and sell carefully assembled, flawlessly structured objects. Elsewhere, organizations such as private exercise gyms and corner coffee shops progressively attune their service ecosystems to adapt to the active role that consumers are taking in today's society. Many organizations draw on technology to take advantage of these changes and arrange their service experiences toward the DIY service encounters that humans seek so that they can participate in co-creation. For such reasons, the creators look at how organizations and individuals stay associated long after resources have been traded and long after recommendations have been introduced (Payne et al. 2008).

To enhance service ecosystem fluidity, other systemic elements may dis-associate with one another. In this feedback loop, a different order may emerge that elicits response from other systemic elements. Multiple disparate feedback loops in a service ecosystem disseminate throughout the system and catalyze clusters of change. Approaches to conventional action consider human activity. These methods can be classified either as structuralist or as agentic. A structuralist perspective stresses the effect of macro-level influences on human life, such as society, politics, or social norms. Fluidity of the service ecosystem increases, and there is possible disruption of prevailing order parameters. In other words, the innovation process gains momentum. To demonstrate a more structuralist perspective, consider Bourdieu's emphasis on the structure of a certain community and his statements on how these structures create a habitus from which behaviors emerge (Bourdieu 1977, p. 77). Similarly, Foucault (1979) takes a structuralist perspective and acknowledges the effect of macro-level influences on individual events but concentrates more on information and control.

The feedback loops that transpire during innovation are thus important for subsequent value propositions that are later introduced to the service ecosystem and are pivotal for moving the innovation process forward. Separately, an agentic orientation stresses the effect of micro-level influences on human behavior, such as personality, emotion, or free will. Transformed beliefs or learned knowledge often emerge in response to value propositions, and these ultimately stimulate feedback loops. When habits, culture, or attitudes change in response to feedback loops, ideas and institutions also change during the innovation process. When systemic elements intermingle, they may influence one another and change the nature of the service ecosystem. Ortner (1984) takes on a more agentic-orientation, discussing how interpersonal abilities can change social structures and how this occurs when participants play the social games of life and eventually exert social impact on the possible trajectories of other events. When a value proposition is introduced to a service ecosystem, it may not always be well-received. In most stable service ecosystems, existing patterns among systemic elements resonate with other existing patterns, and together these are remembered throughout the service ecosystem. However, in service ecosystems that are less stable, the recursivity and feedback loops that occur in response to a value proposition may establish different values and behaviors that then reverberate through the service ecosystem. As innovation is pursued over time, the service ecosystem can change in nature. An action can also refer to the cognitive and affective aspects of social interaction (Schatzki 1996). These collections, events, or actions are often determined by macro-level forces (as observed by those taking a structuralist orientation). But when coordination takes place through shared understanding between participants, Giddens (1979) refers to this as structuration.

Systems are configurations of value which coalesce around humans. By stressing the human dimension of service systems, actions that directly affect service systems by serving as the basic turning points on which service systems are continuously evolving. This can occur at either the micro, meso, or macro levels of the service ecosystem. When systemic elements at each of these levels become harmonized, the service ecosystem becomes more stable over time. Ironically, these pivots are known because they frequently transpire in the mundane events, doings, and happenings (i.e., actions) of daily social life in humanistic forms and places, away from the purview of the business. When these services are nuanced within a particular service structure, they function as a resource hub, as they direct certain individuals, relationships, events, and artifacts around a common attempt to generate value. Ultimately, the other systemic elements that were interconnected with the initial elements then also react to the value proposition and their changed relationship with other systemic elements. This increases the capacity of the service ecosystem to retain a new form by establishing different norms, rules, and beliefs in the service ecosystem. As a result, the service ecosystem is more stable than it was previously. As this happens, the method emerges as a type of action, grounding the service system in a special attempt to build value. Consequently, the service framework adjusts when an action style shifts again (often in response to a new event trigger or parameter in its external environment). In perpetuity, this iterative service repeats itself. This is how configurations for co-creation of product, or service structures, change continually.

Managerial Implications

With respect to plasticity as described in Chap. 2, individual innovators play a significant role in how a service ecosystem adapts to value propositions and innovation efforts. To begin with, individual innovators influence recursivity by often being the ones who stimulate the feedback loops that lead to change among systemic elements. This can increase fluidity in a service ecosystem by allowing the service ecosystem to take new forms. This is because innovators are often bridge spanners, thereby connecting individuals in different subgroups regarding value propositions or innovation efforts. Moreover, innovators tend to associate with diverse sets of individuals who can bring different ideas to different parts of the service ecosystem. This again positively influences fluidity in the service ecosystem.

Individual innovators can also affect the temporality of plasticity buy speeding or slowing the responses of the service ecosystem to value propositions or innovation efforts. For example, if there are more innovators in a particular service ecosystem, then the responses to a value proposition or innovation effort are likely to be faster because innovators are typically open to new ideas and changes. On the other hand, if there are fewer innovators in a service ecosystem, then the responses to value propositions or innovation efforts are likely to be slower since those who do not have an innovation mindset will likely resist change and new ideas. Similarly, in service ecosystems characterized by high numbers of innovators, it is likely that systemic elements will react more in ways that are more complementary to the value propositions and innovation efforts; in other words, the service ecosystem will revert back to synchronicity more quickly. Conversely, for service ecosystems that are characterized by low numbers of innovators, it is likely that systemic elements will not react as positively with respect to new value propositions or innovation efforts and the service ecosystem will either be slow to realign or not realign at all. Finally, because of the persistence of innovators, service ecosystems will likely thrive and continuously evolve. However, service ecosystems characterized with high numbers of innovators are likely to reach this phase faster and with less effort, while service ecosystems characterized with low numbers of innovators are likely to stall in their evolution toward reaching synchronicity.

Ironically, when managers need to stabilize their service ecosystems, they should be aware and conscientious about individuals who demonstrate the traits of innovators. Although innovators are open to change and new ways of thinking, innovators are likely to be seen as "rocking the boat," which is considered to destabilize the service ecosystem. Too much change too quickly is likely to jolt the service ecosystem. Conversely stated, if managers need to open up their service ecosystems in order to make them more resilient or prepare them for change, they should encourage behaviors related to innovation. They should encourage informal dialogue and interaction, risk-taking, and a diverse set of viewpoints.

References

Arnould, E.J., and L.L. Price. 1993. River Magic: Extraordinary Experience and the Extended Service Encounter. *Journal of Human Research* 20: 24–45.

Arnould, E.J., and C.J. Thompson. 2005. Human Culture Theory (CCT): Twenty Years of Research. *Journal of Human Research* 31: 868–882.

Belk, R.W. 1990. The Role of Possessions in Constructing and Maintaining a Sense of Past. *Advances in Human Research* 17: 669–676.

Bitner, M.J. 1992. Servicescapes: The Impact of Physical Surroundings on Customers and Employees. *Journal of Marketing* 56: 57–71.

Bourdieu, P. 1977. *Outline of a Theory of Practice*. Cambridge: Cambridge University Press.

Bournelli, P., A. Makri, and K. Mylonas. 2009. Motor Creativity and Self-Concept. *Creativity Research Journal* 21: 104–110.

Campbell, C. 2005. The Craft Human: Culture, Craft and Consumption in a Postmodern Society. *Journal of Human Culture* 5: 23–42.

Dahl, D.W., and C.P. Moreau. 2007. Thinking Inside the Box: Why Humans Enjoy Constrained Creative Experiences. *Journal of Marketing Research* 44: 357–369.

Deci, E.L., and R.M. Ryan. 2000. The 'What' and 'Why' of Goal Pursuits: Human Needs and the Self-Determination of Behavior. *Psychological Inquiry* 11: 227–268.

Edvardsson, B., B. Enquist, and R. Johnston. 2005. Cocreating Customer Value Through Hyperreality in the Prepurchase Service Experience. *Journal of Service Research* 8 (2): 149–161.

Etgar, M. 2008. A Descriptive Model of the Human Co-production Service. *Journal of the Academy of Marketing Science* 36: 97–108.

Foucault, M. 1979. *Discipline and Punish: The Birth of the Prison*. London: Penguin Books.

Franke, N., and F. Piller. 2004. Value Creation by Toolkits for User Innovation and Design: The Case of the Watch Market. *Journal of Product Innovation Management* 21: 401–415.

Franke, N., P. Keinz, and M. Schreier. 2008. Complementing Mass Customization Toolkits with User Communities: How Peer Input Improves Customer Self-Design. *Journal of Product Innovation Management* 25: 546–559.

Gainer, B. 1995. Ritual and Relationships: Interpersonal Influences on Shared Consumption. *Journal of Business Research* 32: 253–260.

Garzaniti, I., G. Pearce, and J. Stanton. 2011. Building Friendships and Relationships: The Role of Conversation in Hairdressing Service Encounters. *Managing Service Quality* 21: 667–687.

Giddens, A. 1979. *Central Problems in Social Theory*. Oakland: University of California Press.

Grönroos, C., and P. Voima. 2013. Critical Service Logic: Making Sense of Value Creation and Co-creation. *Journal of the Academy of Marketing Science* 41: 133–150.

Kemple, K.M., G.M. David, and Y. Wang. 1996. Preschoolers' Creativity, Shyness, and Self-Esteem. *Creativity Research Journal* 9: 317–326.

Lau, S., C.S. Li, and D. Chu. 2004. Perceived Creativity: Its Relationship to Social Status and Self-Concept Among Chinese High Ability Children. *Creativity Research Journal* 16: 59–67.

McColl-Kennedy, J.R., S.L. Vargo, T.S. Dagger, J.C. Sweeney, and Y. Van Kasteren. 2012. Health Care Customer Value Cocreation Practice Styles. *Journal of Service Research* 15 (4): 370–389.

Muniz, A.M., and T.C. O'Guinn. 2001. Brand Community. *Journal of Human Research* 27: 412–432.

Nicol, J.J., and B.C. Long. 1996. Creativity and Perceived Stress of Female Music: Therapists and Hobbyists. *Creativity Research Journal* 9: 1–10.

Ortner, S.B. 1984. Theory in Anthropology Since the Sixties. *Comparative Studies in Society and History* 26 (1): 126–166.

Payne, A.F., K. Storbacka, and P. Frow. 2008. Managing the Co-creation of Value. *Journal of the Academy of Marketing Science* 36 (1): 83–96.

Pitt, L.F., R.T. Watson, P. Berthon, D. Wynn, and G. Zinkhan. 2006. The Penguin's Window: Corporate Brands from an Open-Source Perspective. *Journal of the Academy of Marketing Science* 34: 115–127.

Prügl, R., and M. Schreier. 2006. Learning from Leading-Edge Customers at The Sims: Opening Up the Innovation Service Using Toolkits. *R&D Management* 36: 237–250.

Reynolds, F. 2004. Conversations About Creativity and Chronic Illness II: Textile Artists Coping with Long-Term Health Problems Reflect on the Creative Service. *Creativity Research Journal* 16: 79–89.

Reynolds, F., K.H. Lim, and S. Prior. 2008. Images of Resistance: A Qualitative Enquiry into the Meanings of Personal Artwork for Women Living with Cancer. *Creativity Research Journal* 20: 211–220.

Ritzer, G. 2014. Prosumption: Evolution, Revolution, or Eternal Return of the Same? *Journal of Human Culture* 14: 3–22.
Rostan, S.M. 2010. Studio Learning: Motivation, Competence, and the Development of Young Art Students' Talent and Creativity. *Creativity Research Journal* 22: 261–271.
Schatzki, T.R. 1996. *Social Practices: A Wittgensteinian Approach to Human Activity and the Social.* Cambridge: Cambridge University Press.
Schembri, S. 2006. Rationalizing Service Logic, or Understanding Services as Experience? *Marketing Theory* 6: 381–392.
Toffler, A. 1980. *The Third Wave.* New York: William Morrow and Company, Inc.
Watson, M., and E. Shove. 2008. Product, Competence, Project and Practice: DIY and the Dynamics of Craft Consumption. *Journal of Human Culture* 8: 69–89.
Xie, C., R.P. Bagozzi, and S.V. Troye. 2008. Trying to Prosume: Toward a Theory of Humans as Co-creators of Value. *Journal of the Academy of Marketing Science* 36: 109–122.
Zausner, T. 1998. When Walls Become Doorways: Creativity, Chaos Theory, and Physical Illness. *Creativity Research Journal* 11: 21–28.

Index

J. D. Chandler, *Innovation, Social Networks, and Service Ecosystems*,
https://doi.org/10.1007/978-3-030-47797-4

The manufacturer's authorised representative in the EU is Springer Nature Customer Service Centre GmbH, Europaplatz 3, 69115 Heidelberg, Germany. If you have any concerns regarding our products, please contact ProductSafety@springernature.com

Printed and bound by CPI Group (UK) Ltd, Croydon, CR0 4YY
05/10/2026
02228154-0001